Clinical Partnerships in Urban Elementary School Settings

Advances in Teaching and Teacher Education

Series Editor

Yeping Li (*Texas A&M University, College Station, USA*)

International Advisory Board

Miriam Ben-Peretz (*University of Haifa, Israel*)
Cheryl J. Craig (*Texas A&M University, USA*)
Jennifer Gore (*University of Newcastle, Australia*)
Stephanie L. Knight (*Southern Methodist University, USA*)
Allen Yuk Lun Leung (*Hong Kong Baptist University, Hong Kong*)
Ian Menter (*University of Oxford, UK*)
Yolanda N. Padrón (*Texas A&M University, USA*)
Hersh C. Waxman (*Texas A&M University, USA*)

VOLUME 4

The titles published in this series are listed at *brill.com/atte*

Clinical Partnerships in Urban Elementary School Settings

An Honest Celebration of the Messy Realities in the Preparation of Teachers

Edited by

Mikkaka Overstreet and Lori Norton-Meier

BRILL
SENSE

LEIDEN | BOSTON

All chapters in this book have undergone peer review.

The Library of Congress Cataloging-in-Publication Data is available online at http://catalog.loc.gov

Typeface for the Latin, Greek, and Cyrillic scripts: "Brill". See and download: brill.com/brill-typeface.

ISSN 2542-9574
ISBN 978-90-04-40850-0 (paperback)
ISBN 978-90-04-40851-7 (hardback)
ISBN 978-90-04-42478-4 (e-book)

Copyright 2020 by Koninklijke Brill NV, Leiden, The Netherlands.
Koninklijke Brill NV incorporates the imprints Brill, Brill Hes & De Graaf, Brill Nijhoff, Brill Rodopi, Brill Sense, Hotei Publishing, mentis Verlag, Verlag Ferdinand Schöningh and Wilhelm Fink Verlag.
All rights reserved. No part of this publication may be reproduced, translated, stored in a retrieval system, or transmitted in any form or by any means, electronic, mechanical, photocopying, recording or otherwise, without prior written permission from the publisher.
Authorization to photocopy items for internal or personal use is granted by Koninklijke Brill NV provided that the appropriate fees are paid directly to The Copyright Clearance Center, 222 Rosewood Drive, Suite 910, Danvers, MA 01923, USA. Fees are subject to change.

This book is printed on acid-free paper and produced in a sustainable manner.

*To the children,
teachers, and administrators who have taught us so much*

Every day I stare in the face of the *messy reality of this work* we call teaching.

It is emotional.

It takes every thought I have about skills, strategies, and expectations but every day I am thankful that I am here.

    DANIELLE, A Teacher Education Major

Contents

Acknowledgements IX
List of Figures and Tables X
Notes on Contributors XI

1 Introduction: Making the Case for the Study of the "Messy Realities" in the Preparation of Teachers   1
 Mikkaka Overstreet and Lori Norton-Meier

2 From Professional Development Schools to P-20 Clinical Teacher Preparation Partnerships: Contemporary Shifts in Addressing the Complex Lives of Students and Educators in Diverse Settings   8
 Ann Larson and Amy Shearer Lingo

3 Mentoring and Third Space in the Academy: The Complexities of Community Engaged Scholarship in Clinical Partnerships   23
 Lori Norton-Meier

4 Navigating Synergic Boundaries: A Collaboration between an Urban Elementary School and a School-Based Mathematics Methods Course   31
 Lateefah Id-Deen, Gabrielle Read-Jasnoff, Shannon Putman and Tim Foster

 Bridging the Theme: Relationships Matter   46
 Mikkaka Overstreet and Lori Norton-Meier

5 Ball Pythons, Bartering and Building Community   47
 Mikkaka Overstreet

 Bridging the Theme: Stories Matter   60
 Mikkaka Overstreet and Lori Norton-Meier

6 From Saviors to Safety Nets: How a Unique Semester Helped Preservice Teachers Think More Deeply about Their Field Placements and Coursework   61
 Tammi R. Davis

 Bridging the Theme: Identity Matters   77
 Mikkaka Overstreet and Lori Norton-Meier

7 Approaching Educational Equity with White Preservice Teachers through an Intersectional Understanding of Self   79
   Bianca Nightengale-Lee

   Bridging the Theme: Reflective Action Matters   92
   Mikkaka Overstreet and Lori Norton-Meier

8 Positioning Students as Writers: A Discourse Analysis in Teacher Education   93
   Emily Zuccaro

   Bridging the Theme: Inquiry Matters   114
   Mikkaka Overstreet and Lori Norton-Meier

9 Perspectives from a First-Year Teacher   115
   Anetria Swanson

   Bridging the Theme: Argument Matters   129
   Mikkaka Overstreet and Lori Norton-Meier

10 Conclusion: Lessons Learned from Research and Practice on the Path to "Ideological Becoming"   130
   Lori Norton-Meier and Mikkaka Overstreet

Acknowledgements

As we put the finishing touches on this volume, we find ourselves extremely grateful for many individuals who helped make this possible. We are so grateful for everyone who has collaborated to bring this book to fruition. Thank you to all of the authors for your unique insights and your willingness to share your triumphs and challenges with such honesty. To the preservice teachers, thank you for taking risks and joining us on this journey. To the administrators and teachers who let us into your schools and classrooms, thank you for the lessons you taught us and for allowing us to become a part of your worlds. To the children, thank you for inspiring us, challenging us, making us laugh, and reminding us why it's all worth it.

Figures and Tables

Figures

2.1   Summary of initiatives and outcomes supported by the Mary K. Oxley Foundation.   18
2.2   Teacher education at the CEHD supported by the Mary K. Oxley Foundation.   19
6.1   Model of prior program.   65
6.2   Model of pilot program.   66
6.3   Overview of findings.   68
7.1   Bashira.   87
10.1 Bridging a new model of "ideological becoming" in clinical teacher preparation.   133

Tables

2.1   College of education and human development at-a-glance.   11
2.2   Conceptual framework aligned with candidate knowledge, skills, and dispositions.   13
6.1   Snapshot of a typical coursework day in our partnership.   67
9.1   School and district teacher retention data (provided by school district).   119
9.2   Seven co-teaching strategies.   126

Notes on Contributors

Tammi R. Davis
is an Assistant Professor of Elementary Education at Missouri State University. For over 30 years she has worked in the field of education as a classroom teacher: as a teacher educator. Her research and teaching focuses on the lives of teachers, teacher education, literacy, narrative inquiry, and reflective practice through the use of a variety of technologies.

Tim Foster
was the principal at Gavin H. Cochran Elementary School in Louisville, KY, and recently retired in 2019. He spent ten years teaching Advanced Placement U.S. Government and Politics at duPont Manual High School. During that time, he received the Gilder-Lehrman Kentucky History Teacher of the Year Award. Tim was an assistant principal at Liberty High School for four years before becoming principal at Cochran. Through his leadership, Tim helped moved the school from the first percentile in state accountability data to a status of proficient school in five short years. Tim approaches education with a student first mindset.

Lateefah Id-Deen
is an Assistant Professor of Mathematics Education in the Department of Early Childhood and Elementary Education at Kennesaw State University. Her research examines vulnerable students' identities and perspectives to enhance student-teacher relationships and their sense of belonging in mathematics classrooms. Additionally, she focuses on ways prospective teachers learn to understand and implement equitable mathematics teaching practices. In addition to research, she teaches mathematics methods courses for prospective elementary mathematics teachers. Her work reflects her passion for creating equitable learning environments for students of color in mathematics classrooms.

Ann Larson
is the Assistant to the President focused on P-20 initiatives and former Dean of the College of Education and Human Development at the University of Louisville. Dr. Larson was a middle and secondary classroom teacher for 13 years in Kansas. Dr. Larson's research areas are curriculum theory and studies, teacher education and development, professional development schools, and English education. She has been actively engaged in leadership roles that have supported success in national and state accreditations (NCATE, CAEP, and EPSB)

of educator preparation programs and professional development schools, and has been active in English education. Dr. Larson currently serves as a member of AACTE's Executive Board.

Bianca Nightengale-Lee
is an Assistant Professor at Florida Atlantic University in the department of Curriculum, Culture, & Educational Inquiry. Dr. Nightengale-Lee has taught for 15 years in urban, suburban, and rural settings, which has grounded her non-traditional approach to literacy pedagogy for culturally and linguistically diverse students. Her research situates in critical literacy and intersectionality as it relates to anti-discriminatory and inclusive educational practice. As a critical researcher, Nightengale-Lee develops courses which seek to critique, resist, and re-design traditional ideologies of how literacy is taught, and learned, to re-frame the ways we engage students of color in literacy instruction.

Lori Norton-Meier
is a Professor of Literacy Education and Interim Director of the Interdisciplinary Early Childhood Research Center at the University of Louisville. She taught in the public schools for seven years in an inner-city environment where many of her students lived in poverty and for whom English was a second language. Dr. Norton-Meier's areas of interest include early childhood education, cross-disciplinary literacy practices in mathematics, and science, teacher as researcher, mixed methods research, case studies of teachers and young learners, both preservice and advanced teacher education, clinical partnerships, and a particular emphasis on equity, access and inclusive practices.

Mikkaka Overstreet
is an Assistant Professor at East Carolina University. Her research focuses on preservice and in-service teacher learning and change, particularly as related to enacting culturally responsive pedagogical practices. Her current research centers on integrating culturally responsive practices as content in literacy methods courses in order to prioritize and centralize this work in teacher education. Additionally, she is collaborating on research projects focused on recruitment and retention of teachers of color at various stages in the educational pipeline, on the integration of arts and literacy in schools serving diverse populations, and on engaging preservice teachers with culturally responsive pedagogy.

Shannon Putman
is a Teacher in Residence at Cochran Elementary School in Louisville, Kentucky. She spent eight years teaching the multi-modal communication special

NOTES ON CONTRIBUTORS   XIII

education classroom. She also spent two years as the learning and behavior disorder resource teacher. While working over the last three years as the teacher in residence, Shannon has focused on supporting the professional development relationship between Cochran Elementary and the University of Louisville. Her doctoral work explores the use of virtual reality technology as educational interventions.

Gabrielle Read-Jasnoff
is a Curriculum and Instruction doctoral candidate at the University of Louisville in Louisville, Kentucky. Her main areas of research include mathematics and technology education, and teacher preparation. Her professional educational experiences include middle-secondary mathematics teacher, technology education instructor, and digital content and technology integration specialist. Gabrielle's passion includes helping current and future educators improve their craft by integrating technology into their teaching and learning.

Amy Shearer Lingo
is the Interim Dean of the College of Education and Human Development at the University of Louisville. Previously, she was appointed as the Associate Dean for Academic Affairs and Unit Effectiveness beginning July 2015. Her research interests are academic interventions for P-12 students with or at risk for disabilities. Dr. Lingo has been heavily engaged in P-12 schools in Kentucky through her teaching, research and service. In addition, she has continuously served as a Teacher Educator with the Kentucky Teacher Internship Program (KTIP) since 1999 to support the induction and retention of new teachers in Kentucky P-12 school classrooms.

Anetria Swanson
is a Resource Teacher in the Human Resources department of Jefferson County Public Schools. She oversees student teacher and field experience placements and assists in the district's teacher recruitment and retention efforts. Anetria earned a Master of Arts in Teaching and a Master's Degree in K-12 School Counseling from the University of Louisville. She has worked with a team of resource teachers to develop a new elementary social studies curriculum promoting civic knowledge and engagement. Anetria is an adjunct lecturer for the University of Louisville, where she is pursuing a doctoral degree in curriculum and instruction.

Emily Zuccaro
is an Assistant Professor at Eastern Kentucky University with an emphasis in Literacy Education. Her dissertation examines the teaching of English to

Congolese refugees. She currently leads the Kentucky Reading Project at the University of Louisville; previously, she taught third grade in Houston, Texas, second grade in Monterrey, Mexico, and literacy methods courses at the University of Louisville.

CHAPTER 1

Introduction: Making the Case for the Study of the "Messy Realities" in the Preparation of Teachers

Mikkaka Overstreet and Lori Norton-Meier

Abstract

Within the field of education there is a noted gap between research and practice, between K-12 schools and universities and, in teacher education, between educational theories and practical classroom application (Dieker et al., 2014; Durnan, 2016). Clinical partnerships between schools and universities demonstrate one method for bridging these gaps (Howell, Carpenter, & Jones, 2013; Johnson, 2010). These partnerships ideally bring university faculty and students into K-12 schools for the mutual benefit of both parties. Unfortunately, such partnerships are often one-sided with universities reaping the most benefits. In a complex climate of education reform, it is imperative that these partnerships are truly collaborative and involve all stakeholders in planning, implementation, facilitation, and evaluation in order to be successful and effectively utilize a shrinking pool of resources (Howell, Carpenter, & Jones, 2013). Readers of this chapter will: (1) be introduced to the stories of teacher educators working through the "messy reality" of engaging in clinical teaching work; (2) gain insight to the complexity of the relationships with community, university, and schools and the individuals who seek to establish and/or nurture equitable learning environments for students; (3) understand the power of qualitative research as a tool for telling stories about this messy work as well as discuss the necessity in valuing such efforts among higher education.

Keywords

clinical partnerships – teacher preparation – professional narratives

> Sometimes reality is too complex. Stories give it form.
> JEAN LUC GODARD, film director, screenwriter, film critic

∴

We cannot create a world we can't imagine and stories are the engines of our imaginations.

JOSH STEARNS

∴

1   Introduction

Humans understand the world through the power of story. Neuroscience tells us that the human brain works diligently to create narratives to help people navigate the complexities of our experiences (Wilson, 2002). We remember stories infinitely more easily than we recall facts and figures. We rely on stories to make sense of new knowledge and experiences by connecting to the stories we already know.

Thus, to make research both useful and enjoyable to readers, the best researchers construct narratives that turn scientific phenomena into accessible information (Wilson, 2002). By offering many stories on a given phenomenon, we can begin to understand it and to make decisions about how to use that understanding—in this case for the improvement of the field of education.

Join us. We are going to tell you a story.

2   The Who and the Why

Once upon a time there was a group of teacher educators. They came from very different walks of life and were at very different stages in their careers. Yet somehow their paths had led them all to one institution and, at that institution, they all worked with preservice teachers. But they didn't just work within the confines of their ivory tower; they took their students out into the community.

The field needs their stories. Since 2010, when the National Council for Accreditation of Teacher Education (NCATE) Blue Ribbon Panel proclaimed clinical partnerships as a foundational component of a high-quality teacher education program, many universities have added or expanded partnerships. Due to the widespread adoption of the concept, however, a great deal of variation remains in the structure, expectations, and language of these partnerships (AACTE, 2018). The field needs clear *examples* of what clinical partnerships are, as well as what they should be. According to Durnan (2016), "What is needed in the near term is a broader inventory of examples demonstrating why the effort makes sense and why the reward is worth the risk" (p. 710, emphasis added).

3 The Setting

This is a timely story in today's context; "clinical practice offers a lens through which to understand the problems of practice that currently face the profession, stemming from factors such as demographic changes, poverty, and teacher shortages" (AACTE, 2018, p. 8). As "baby boomers" retire and complex factors converge to create a decreased interest in the teaching profession, it is more imperative than ever to adequately prepare the next generation of teachers so that they are equipped with the skills and mindsets necessary to persist in the field. First-year teachers are regularly placed in difficult contexts: high poverty schools where children would most benefit from experienced practitioners. Poor children are twice as likely than their economically advantaged counterparts to be assigned first-year teachers (Haycock, 2004). Their schools typically have very high turnover rates, about 50% higher than more affluent schools, meaning that our most needy students are being exposed to beginning teachers year after year. Logically, teachers improve as they gain experience; unfortunately, it is students who suffer while first-year teachers learn on the job. To mitigate this gap between research and practice, preservice teachers need contextualized field experiences in diverse settings (Laman, Miller, & Lopez-Robinson, 2012).

Our program provides these type of contextualized field experiences. Strategically situated in the city's poorest neighborhoods, our partnership schools offer preservice teachers opportunities to work with economically, linguistically, and racially diverse students. These schools are located in our state's largest school district, which serves over 100,000 students, making it one of the thirty largest districts in the country. Over 50% of the population are students of color. Approximately 60% qualify for free or reduced lunch.

The clinical partnership work of the university serves an enactment of its commitment to social justice. According to the college of education's conceptual framework,

> We believe that advocacy is a motivation for service and a support for change and that it is essential to strengthening a dynamic, democratic society. We demonstrate our commitment to social and human equity in our teaching, research, professional practices, relationships with others, and actions undertaken outside the college. (COE conceptual framework)

Those actions include hands-on engagement in designated professional development schools, with an aim to "eliminate disparities in education, health, economic development, and human/social services" (COE conceptual framework).

4   The Problem

Leading teacher education researchers and organizations agree that "clinical practice and partnership are central to high-quality teacher preparation" (AACTE, 2018, p. 9). In order to effectively prepare teacher candidates for the demands of today's classrooms, programs must offer a balance of rigorous academic content with opportunities to observe and apply pedagogical practice under the guidance of skilled university-based and school-based educators (Laman, Miller, & Lopez-Robinson, 2012; NCATE, 2010). Providing such balanced programs is a complicated endeavor. Challenges include finding suitable placements for teacher candidates, navigating scheduling difficulties and ideological differences between school districts and universities, defining roles between school and university personnel, and much more.

The field experience component is crucial to teacher preparation. Preservice teachers (PSTs) commonly struggle to transfer knowledge and skills from the university setting into the classroom (Dawson & Lignugaris/Kraft, 2017; Dieker, Rodriguez, Lignugaris/Kraft, Hynes, & Hughes, 2014). Clinical partnerships provide a much-needed mechanism to allow PSTs more time working in real classroom settings with real students, thus providing the necessary experience to prepare them to persist in the profession (Guha, Hyler, & Darling-Hammond, 2017).

The American Association of Colleges for Teacher Education (AACTE) Clinical Practice Commission (2018) defines clinical practice as

> Teacher candidates' work in authentic educational settings and engagement in the pedagogical work of the profession of teaching, closely integrated with educator preparation course work and supported by a formal school-university partnership. Clinical practice is a specific form of what is traditionally known as fieldwork. (p. 11)

This work "joins the needs of a college or university and local PK-12 schools in the preparation of highly effective educators to meet the needs of all learners" (p. 4) by "preparing teacher candidates through an interwoven structure of academic learning and the professional application of that knowledge—under the guidance of skilled school-based and university-based teacher educators" (p. 6). Despite the agreement on the necessity of clinical practice and the call for more consistency in its enactment, educational leaders agree that these partnerships must vary in consideration of local contexts (AACTE, 2018). The careful balance between large-scale cohesion and localized responsiveness will only be achieved through the sharing of stories—stories from those doing this work in a variety of contexts and with varying outcomes.

5   Our Solution

We by no means have all of the answers. We don't even have most of the answers. What we do have within these pages is the findings of a diverse group of teacher educators who have been doing this work. Each scholar presents her case story—a very specific professional narrative and documentary account of a specific experience in a messy, complicated space of working collaboratively in elementary school settings. To help connect these case stories, we offer a text feature we call *"Bridging the theme"* between each case study and in our final chapter we will return to the bridges to pull together and present a new model for consideration when engaging clinical partnerships in the preparation of teachers.

We begin this book here in Chapter 1 by setting the stage for the reader and situating our case studies in a context of theory, practice, and structure to help the reader engage uniquely with this text. In Chapter 2, the administrative leaders of our college, Ann Larson and Amy Shearer Lingo give an overview of the clinical partnership model at our institution—how it began, how it has evolved, and how it situates within a larger discussion of the profession's development of the preparation of teachers situated in actual K-12 school settings. After the overview presented in the previous chapter, Lori Norton-Meier follows by reflecting on the challenges of not only doing this work but mentoring new scholars and cooperating teachers to be willing to take up this work. Lori Norton-Meier posits that the theorizing around the need to create a "third space" for the children we work with in classrooms also needs to happen for the adults who are working to support the development of new teachers. In Chapter 4, Lateefah Id-Deen, alongside her graduate assistant and partnership school staff, explores the complex interplay between research-based mathematics teaching practices, public school governance (and its impact on schools' instructional decisions), school-based experiences for preservice teachers, and the multitude of other factors that make or break school-university partnerships. In the next chapter, Mikkaka Overstreet adds to this discussion, examining similar factors (centered on literacy rather than math), while providing specifics about the ground-level effort required of school-based methods instructors involved in university-school partnerships. Tammi Davis then takes us deeper into another perspective, focusing on the experiences of preservice teachers in school-based literacy methods courses as they negotiate the goals and beliefs they bring to the setting, the theories and practices encouraged in the methods course, and the reality of applying both in their work with children. In light of the deficit perspectives often revealed when preservice teachers begin to spend time in K-12 classrooms, Bianca Nightengale-Lee shares specific lessons from her school-based literacy methods course that sought to counteract deficit narratives and encourage educational equity through an intersectional approach to understanding identity. Similarly, Emily Zuccaro examines the knowledge, beliefs, and values of preservice teachers in school-based literacy methods courses, using discourse analysis to elucidate their thinking and the intersection of their worlds as college students and future educators. Next, Anetria Swanson connects preservice experiences to in-service practice through a case study of a first-year teacher, exploring the factors from teacher education programs and early career supports from schools and districts (or lack thereof) that might influence retention. Each chapter includes recommendations for educators interested in creating partnerships and implications for future research and improvement. We, the editors, return in the conclusion to bring this story to a close by offering a new model for the preparation of teachers along with additional suggestions, connections, and conjectures.

References

American Association of Colleges for Teacher Education (AACTE) Clinical Practice Commission. (2018). *A pivot toward clinical practice, its Lexicon, and the renewal of educator preparation.*

Dawson, M., & Lignugaris/Kraft, B. (2017). Meaningful practice: Generalizing foundation teaching skills from TLE TeachlivE™ to the classroom. *Teacher Education and Special Education, 40*(1), 26–50.

Dieker, L., Rodriguez, J., Lignugaris/Kraft, B., Hynes, M., & Hughes, C. (2014). The potential of simulated environments in teacher education: Current and future possibilities. *Teacher Education and Special Education, 37*(1), 21–33.

Guha, R., Hyler, M., & Darling-Hammond, L. (2017). The teacher residency: A practical path to recruitment and retention. *The Education Digest, 83*(2), 38.

Haycock, K. (2004). The elephant in the living room. *Brookings Papers on Education Policy, 2004*(1), 229–247.

Laman, T. T., Miller, E. T., & López-Robertson, J. (2012). Noticing and naming as social practice: Examining the relevance of a contextualized field-based early childhood literacy methods course. *Journal of Early Childhood Teacher Education, 33*(1), 3–18.

National Council for Accreditation of Teacher Education (NCATE) Blue Ribbon Panel on Clinical Preparation and Partnerships for Improved Student Learning. (2010). *Transforming teacher education through clinical practice: A national strategy to prepare effective teachers*. Washington, DC: NCATE. Retrieved from http://www.ncate.org/LinkClick.aspx?fileticket=zzeiB1OoqPk%3D

Wilson, E. O. (2002). The power of story. *American Educator, 26*(1), 8–11.

CHAPTER 2

From Professional Development Schools to P-20 Clinical Teacher Preparation Partnerships: Contemporary Shifts in Addressing the Complex Lives of Students and Educators in Diverse Settings

Ann Larson and Amy Shearer Lingo

Abstract

In this chapter, two administrators give an overview of the historical underpinnings related to the growth of clinical partnership models both from a broad perspective and from a local perspective. This chapter sets the stage by describing not only the historical events that brought the six emerging scholars to this location to do this work in schools but also contextualizing the current climate in regards to regulations, standards, and efforts to reform education both locally, in the state, and beyond particularly emphasizing the complex lives of the students we teach in this diverse, urban setting.

Keywords

teacher preparation – urban education – school-university partnerships

1   Context: Setting the Stage for Clinical Teacher Preparation

As administrators and faculty working in teacher preparation at the University of Louisville (English education, curriculum studies and special education, learning and behavior disorders, respectively), we would like to sincerely acknowledge the many, diverse P-12 students, faculty, staff, alumni, and district, school, community and state agency partners who participate in our national and state accredited programs that prepare teachers and other school professionals for the Commonwealth of Kentucky and beyond.

The University of Louisville (UofL) in Louisville, KY traces its origins to the Jefferson Seminary, which was chartered in 1798 and opened in 1813. The

University added the School of Education in 1968, which became the College of Education and Human Development (CEHD) in 2001. UofL has a Carnegie classification of institutions of higher education as a Research 1 (highest research activity) university and has earned for two recent review cycles the Carnegie Foundation for the Advancement of Teaching's highest rating in the area of community engagement. It has been accredited since 1915, and is authorized to award associate, bachelor, masters, specialist, doctoral, and professional degrees.

UofL and CEHD strive to foster and sustain an environment of inclusiveness that empowers individuals to achieve their highest potential without fear of prejudice or bias. The University partners with Jefferson County Public Schools (JCPS), Louisville's large urban school district, ranked the 29th largest district nationally, with approximately 101,000 K-12 students, and Louisville Metro government. The University launched the Signature Partnership Initiative (SPI) (University of Louisville, Signature Partnership, 2018) within the last decade to improve education, healthcare, social services, and economic opportunity in West Louisville. West Louisville is comprised of nearly a dozen neighborhoods, where the majority of UofL's SPI public schools reside and from where children and adolescents attend or are bused within JCPS to achieve diverse student representation in all district schools. Like other universities located in close proximity to such urban centers, UofL states as a part of its mission the goal of making a positive and sustaining impact in addressing community needs. Although simply stated, the aim is comprehensive: "The university is drawing upon the expertise and energy of faculty, staff, and students from every school and college of UofL to deal with the quality of life issues affecting our community."

As faculty within the CEHD, our roles have been to apply an established and continuously improving clinical model of teacher education with our school partners, with the most focused efforts in designated SPI schools. Guided by the principles detailed in NCATE's (now the Council for the Accreditation of Educator Preparation, CAEP) *Blue Ribbon Panel Report* (2010) and in numerous chapters of the seminal *Handbook of Research on Teacher Education: Enduring Questions in Changing Contexts*, third edition (2008), our current reform efforts in teacher education focus on the role of clinical preparation and partnerships between higher education and P-12 to prepare teachers for improved learning and achievement for all students. AACTE's Clinical Practice Commission report, *A Pivot Toward Clinical Practice, its Lexicon, and the Renewal of Educator Preparation*, cautions that there is a "cacophony of perspectives" across the nation's teacher preparation programs regarding what constitutes clinical practice. The commission calls on the field of teacher education to pivot from its "divergent understandings of terms, structures and quality" and to embrace a shared direction going forward. AACTE's Clinical Practice Commission's report strategically followed NCATE's Blue Ribbon Panel Report (2010) and identifies elements of what makes clinical teacher preparation programs successful in order to assist the field in strengthening programs. The AACTE report names ten essential proclamations for effective clinical preparation, each with its own tenets and a narrative description. Topics including pedagogy, partnership infrastructure, valuing expertise and collaboration among professionals, moral imperatives and research-derived evidence are shared and a strong recommendation for the field of teacher education to use a common lexicon to define "the concepts and entities" in clinical preparation." The report also recommends a common lexicon to define the concepts and entities engaged in clinical preparation, identifies model protocols, proposes solutions to common roadblocks, and highlights relevant research to aid partners in enhancing programs.

The transformation of teacher education through clinical partnerships (Darling-Hammond, 2006) forms the organizing structure within which all stakeholders commit to the recruitment, admission, preparation, assessment, and continuing development of teachers who effectively enable the learning of all students in all contexts (CAEP, 2018; Darling-Hammond, 1999). In 2014, a team of CEHD faculty and administrators co-edited a theme issue and published with others nationwide in a theme issue of the *Peabody Journal of Education* (2014), "Clinical Partnerships in Teacher Education: Perspectives, Practices, and Outcomes," to address the critical topic of these models across national higher education institutions that prepare teachers.

In this chapter, we expand on the further development of our work in a clinical model of teacher preparation. There continue to be fine examples of exemplary programs across the country with histories and success in partnership endeavors, shared opportunities, challenges and policy implications to provide possibilities for student learning. The extensive literature cited in AACTE's (2010) policy brief illuminates the benefits of teacher preparation linked to practice in authentic school settings is a key and contemporary theme in the field that cannot be ignored. The clinical preparation of teachers through rich clinical partnerships is what a high-quality program in teacher preparation must be and is essential to transforming teacher preparation and the educational experiences of P-12 students.

Thus, our university's commitment to community engagement and development has aligned well with our college's attempt to honor and enact the partnership-based principles advocated in NCATE's *Blue Ribbon Panel Report* (2010). Understanding the CEHD's long and substantial commitments to school and district partnerships in an urban setting through general education and special education in teacher preparation programs is an important part of the story we share in this chapter.

TABLE 2.1　College of education and human development at-a-glance

CEHD students and staff	Educator preparation programs in CEHD
– ~3100 undergraduate, masters, post-master's and doctoral students – 100 full-time faculty – Part-time faculty, other unit faculty, clinical educators – Program and administrative staff members, student workers, graduate assistants, and several post-doctoral fellows	*Early Childhood and Elementary Education* – Birth through grade 5 *Middle and Secondary Education* – 5–12, K-12, 5–9, and 9–12 *Special Education* – Initial certification and advanced degree programs serving a diverse range of disabilities age 0-21 *Counseling and Human Development* – Counselor education *Educational Leadership, Evaluation, and Organizational Development* – Career and technical education, educational administration, and educational leadership and organizational development *Health and Sports Sciences* – P-12 physical and health education

1.1　*Transformation through Collaboration*

The Nystrand Center of Excellence in Education (NCEE), named for former Dean Ray Nystrand, is dedicated to the continual support of educational excellence for all students through innovative thinking, transformational educator preparation, professional development, and supportive learning environments. The purpose of the NCEE, one of five Commonwealth Centers of Excellence and the only one in education in Kentucky, is to develop, implement and study collaborative efforts to improve teaching. The NCEE's key initiatives include CEHD's clinical model of educator preparation and UofL SPI collaborations (NCEE, 2018). The NCEE also houses CEHD's Multicultural Teacher Recruitment Program (MTRP). MTRP, in collaboration with the University of Louisville, Jefferson County Public Schools (JCPS) and the Ohio Valley Educational Cooperative (OVEC) since its inception in 1985, endeavors to proactively alleviate teacher shortages at all levels by increasing teacher candidates of color so that the nation, Kentucky, and the Louisville metropolitan area reflect contemporary demographics and promote teacher capacity and social justice in teacher education and P-12 field and clinical settings (Grant & Agosto, 2008).

1.2 *Shaping Tomorrow: Ideas to Action*

The CEHD's conceptual framework (University of Louisville, College of Education and Human Development, 2018) reflects a commitment to functioning as one college with interdisciplinary and cross-disciplinary elements. CEHD faculty, staff, and administrators work toward the common goals of providing high-quality programs for all students and enhancing the college's capacity in research, scholarship, and extramural funding. *Shaping Tomorrow: Ideas to Action*, CEHD's conceptual framework with its three constructs of inquiry, action, and advocacy which frames our work incorporates a shared vision of various stakeholders, including university, school, and community partners.

1.3 *Shared Values and Beliefs for Educator Preparation*

Our conceptual framework has direct relation to the preparation of teacher candidates to be exemplary professional practitioners and scholars; to generating, using, and disseminating knowledge about teaching, learning, health promotion, disease prevention, policy development, and leadership in public and private sector organizations; and to collaborating with others to solve critical human problems in a diverse global community. The current conceptual framework has evolved over the past decade; it is rooted in the bioecological model of development (Bronfenbrenner & Morris, 1998), which says that individuals develop through active interactions within and between the contexts surrounding them and that they function as essential parts of the larger community and society. The bioecological model notes that the environment is comprised of various "systems" (those with direct influence on the development of an individual such as teachers and families and those with indirect influence such as community organizations). In CEHD's conceptual framework, these systems are represented by the constructs of: (a) inquiry: occurs when faculty and students engage in the conduct of education science to maximize understanding of what works in education, for whom it works, and why; (b) action: occurs when learning environments are created and staffed with well-prepared professionals who are committed to forming the best possible environments for children; and (c) advocacy: community members and organizations (public and private) create environments in which inquiry and action occur, with the goal of promoting the highest levels of learning, ethical behavior, and well-being for all children, adults, and families.

TABLE 2.2 Conceptual framework aligned with candidate knowledge, skills, and dispositions

Conceptual framework constructs	Inquiry	Action	Advocacy
Constructs as learned and applied	Research	Practice	Service
Constructs reflected in students	Critical thinkers	Problem solvers	Professional leaders
Unit dispositions reflected in students	Exhibits a disposition to inform practice through inquiry and reflection	Exhibits a disposition to critique and change practice through content, pedagogical, and professional knowledge	Exhibits a disposition to affirm principles of social justice and equity and a commitment to making a positive difference

CEHD professionals in education and human development create an environment of learning for all candidates by designing instruction that is engaging, encourages all students to persist, encourages critical thinking and effective communication, and honors diversity. College administration and faculty value evidence-based instructional decisions and believe that results of scientifically based research must guide the professional practice of leaders, counselors, and other professionals in school settings, clinics, non-profit agencies, and businesses. It is across this backdrop that CEHD prepares candidates in teacher preparation programs.

1.4   *A Powerful Influence: Council for the Accreditation of Educator Preparation, Standard 2*

The Council for the Accreditation of Educator Preparation's (CAEP, 2018) Standard 2, Clinical Partnerships and Practice, provides a standards-based framework and helps drive CEHD's university and school partnerships as an essential foundation for our programs which prepare initial and advanced teacher preparation. CAEP standard 2 asserts that "The provider ensures that effective partnerships and high-quality clinical practice are central to preparation so that candidates develop the knowledge, skills, and professional dispositions necessary to demonstrate positive impact on all P-12 students' learning and development" (CAEP, 2018). There are three components of CAEP standard 2 for educator preparation providers:

1.4.1   Partnerships for Clinical Preparation

Partners co-construct mutually beneficial P-12 school and community arrangements, including technology-based collaborations, for clinical preparation and share responsibility for continuous improvement of candidate preparation. Partnerships for clinical preparation can follow a range of forms, participants, and functions. They establish mutually agreeable expectations for candidate entry, preparation, and exit; ensure that theory and practice are linked; maintain coherence across clinical and academic components of preparation; and share accountability for candidate outcomes.

1.4.2   Clinical Educators

Partners co-select, prepare, evaluate, support, and retain high-quality clinical educators, both provider- and school-based, who demonstrate a positive impact on candidates' development and P-12 student learning and development. In collaboration with their partners, providers use multiple indicators and appropriate technology-based applications to establish, maintain, and refine criteria for selection, professional development, performance evaluation, continuous improvement, and retention of clinical educators in all clinical placement settings.

1.4.3   Clinical Experiences

The provider works with partners to design clinical experiences of sufficient depth, breadth, diversity, coherence, and duration to ensure that candidates demonstrate their developing effectiveness and positive impact on all students' learning and development. Clinical experiences, including technology-enhanced learning opportunities, are structured to have multiple performance-based assessments at key points within the program to demonstrate candidates' development of the knowledge, skills, and professional dispositions, as delineated in [CAEP] Standard 1, that are associated with a positive impact on the learning and development of all P-12 students.

To provide quality assurances in meeting CAEP Standard 2 and its three components, UofL and CEHD continuously seek to ensure that effective partnerships and high quality clinical practice are central to the preparation of candidates in all educator preparation programs (Alter & Coggshall, 2009). Placements are co-constructed and arranged in collaboration with school district partners, including JCPS and OVEC districts, up to 16 possible collaborative venues. Advisory boards and other district and school partners to CEHD provide input to ensure that preservice teacher candidates, at bachelor's and master's certification levels, experience rich, student demographic diversity when placed in several of four unique school settings: Signature Partnership School, Clinical Partnership School, Professional Development School, or Partner School, defined based on the type of partnership and the University's structures.

Additionally, CEHD's "Ideas to Action" Developmental Teacher Preparation Model provides a framework for candidate experiences to culminate in a professional semester that is based on CAEP's clinical model of teacher preparation. Our model focuses on the application and demonstration of candidates' learning across the Kentucky Teacher Performance Standards (KTPS) (Kentucky Teacher Performance Standards, 2018; Kentucky Department of Education, 2018). Candidates complete coursework and field experiences to ensure that theory and practice are linked. CEHD's Office of Educator Development and Clinical Practice (OEDCP) facilitates the guiding constructs of CAEP Standard 2 between partner schools and the university with articulations being agreed upon and co-constructed on an annual basis. A formal memorandum of understanding is created for schools in clinical experiences and is updated yearly. Candidate placements are contingent on identifying a qualified mentor and considering candidates' previous placements and experiences, personal/work connections, and experiences with diverse learners. Candidate aspirations for district and school employment are also considered.

University liaisons, clinical faculty, and tenure stream faculty serve as supervisors who work in clinical settings. These individuals communicate regularly with school based clinical educators both virtually and in-person. Feedback is discussed during university supervisor meetings held at least four times annually and shared with CEHD department chairs, assistant chairs, and/or an OEDCP field and advisory ad hoc committee. Our continuous assessment system also provides data on candidate performance (knowledge, skills and dispositions) within and across programs that inform decision-making and program improvements.

JCPS and OVEC districts have collaborated with UofL and other universities to reach teachers who are required to complete a co-teaching training. Furthermore, orientations for clinical experiences bring candidates, cooperating teachers, university supervisors and teacher education faculty together in formal settings to clarify roles and responsibilities of the professional clinical experience. Cooperating teachers receive information about a tuition benefit offered for hosting a student teacher, which allows the cooperating teacher to pursue advanced graduate study at UofL in one of many programs, specializations, endorsements or certificates.

1.5 CEEDAR *Initiative as a State-wide Collaboration in Teacher Preparation Reform*

Several years ago, CEHD was chosen to participate in a collaborative opportunity with three other Kentucky higher education teacher preparation institutions, state agencies, and P-12 district-school partners. Through this new partnership, we have expanded our clinical model of teacher education within the University of Florida's Collaboration for Effective Educator Development, Accountability and Reform (CEEDAR) Center and its partner cohorts. CEEDAR is funded by the U.S. Department of Education, Office of Special Education Programs, and is in partnership with the Council for Exceptional Children (CEC) to help states and institutions of higher education reform their teacher and leader preparation programs, revise licensure standards to align with reforms, refine personnel evaluation systems, and realign policy structures and professional learning systems (CEEDAR, 2018).

As a member of CEEDAR's Kentucky partnership, Kentucky's CEEDAR work, is heavily focused on the incorporation of evidence-based practices (EBPs) in educator preparation programs (EPPs). Kentucky is currently developing a common knowledge base and coherent language or lexicon of EBPs at the state, district, and university/college levels. In addition, EPPs are co-constructing partnerships with districts to ensure that preservice educators are provided intentional, high-quality field/clinical experiences in diverse settings where EBPs are coherent and linked. EPPs are using the innovation configurations (ICs) provided by CEEDAR to build consensus regarding EBPs and high-leverage practices (HLPs) among faculty and integrate EBPs and HLPs into all coursework across programs (Ball & Forzani, 2011).

Kentucky is also identifying ways to leverage CEEDAR to revise preparation standards for EPPs, aligning the CEEDAR work CAEP standards to increase sustainability and impact, and will review educator licensure standards to identify areas for recommended changes (e.g., grade level restrictions on content levels, dual certification). Through our CEEDAR work, Kentucky intends to build the capacity of EPPs to use data from the state's data system to engage in continual program improvement. CEHD is enthusiastic about being part of this national reform initiative and the rich opportunities it provides to improve our teacher preparation programs, again, in partnership with selective others.

2 A Generous Donor Gift to Support and Enhance a Clinical Model of Teacher Preparation: The University's Signature Partnership Initiative

The CEHD received a generous gift from the Mary K. Oxley Foundation in 2012 for $1,000,000 followed in 2015 with another $5,000,000 with an additional commitment of $2,500,000 from the UofL Foundation. The gifts support University and CEHD work with the Jefferson County Public Schools (JCPS) through the Signature Partnership Initiative (SPI).

The Mary K. Oxley Foundation funds further support the University and CEHD's efforts to ensure that high quality teachers are reaching and teaching every student. The funds support strategies to recruit high quality educators to SPI schools and provide teachers with engaging, job-embedded professional development that ensures their ability to teach effectively in diverse, high-need and urban school settings. Funding from the Mary K. Oxley Foundation supports five strategies that are necessary in achieving UofL and CEHD SPI goals:

– Creating cohorts for the National Board for Professional Teaching Standards Certification Program (NBPTS), a program that national studies indicate increases teacher effectiveness and student academic achievement;
– Providing comprehensive job-embedded professional development based on student achievement data, presentations at national conferences to disseminate the progress and outcomes on identified school-based initiatives, and UofL faculty conducting professional development with SPI teachers in schools;
– Creating a Clinical Fellows Program with designated funding in the 2017–2018 and 2018–2019 school years for teachers and leaders in SPI schools to continue the process of advancing their leadership certifications;
– Establishing a Teacher in Residence (a district employed certified teacher who serves as the CEHD's SPI faculty liaison, provides ongoing embedded professional development, supports content methods teacher candidates and student teachers, collaborates on research, and more);
– Providing summer learning opportunities to prevent students' learning regression while school is not in session.

The initiatives supported by these funds are multi-faceted and extensive. For a summary of some of the outcomes that have been achieved for CEHD's teacher candidates in their clinical experiences and P-12 inservice teachers and the students they serve (Kini & Podolsky, 2016) through the foundation gift, see Figure 2.1.

NBCT
- From 2010-2016 supported 36 nationally board-certified teachers in the SPI schools
- Directly impacted approximately 1,000 P-12 students each year (average of 30 students per teacher)

Comprehensive Professional Development
- Provides comprehensive job-embedded professional development based on student achievement data
- Supports presentations at national conferences to disseminate the progress and outcomes on identified school-based
- Supports work of Teacher in Residence (a district employed certified teacher who serves as the CEHD's SPI faculty liaison)

Summer Learning Opportunities
- Summer Boost program created to to prevent students' learning regression while school is not in session
- Hundreds of students receive support each summer in the form of transportation, meals, educational field trips, and learning materials

FIGURE 2.1   Summary of initiatives and outcomes supported by the Mary K. Oxley Foundation

2.1 Funding for a Clinical Model of Teacher Education

Too often, one of the missing components in teacher education is the authentic opportunity to learn to teach in diverse, high-needs schools (Bettini & Young, 2017). Through the Mary K. Oxley Foundation gift, UofL CEHD preservice teachers are learning in school contexts to serve children who come from high poverty, underserved neighborhoods. The Mary K. Oxley Foundation gift and its primary components (NBCT, Teachers in Residence, a Summer Boost program, and ongoing professional development) elevate this work to a higher level because many of the gaps endemic to urban schools in the U.S. are addressed through the SPI—providing the type of support necessary to create classrooms where student teachers have direct access to experienced and highly qualified teachers who support student teachers in learning how to link theory to practice to address the learning needs of students from diverse groups and with an array of learning needs (Guha, Hyler, & Darling-Hammond, 2016).

The Mary K. Oxley Foundation has greatly benefited CEHD student teachers. The majority of UofL CEHD teacher preparation students will take their content methods courses (literacy, mathematics, social studies, and science) in an SPI school. Figure 2.2 outlines numerical data related to teacher education at the CEHD as supported by the Mary K. Oxley Foundation.

Using a conservative estimate of 90 percent completion rate among teacher candidates participating in this donor and foundation funded initiative and an average first year salary of $49,000 in Kentucky, the economic impact of the teacher candidates served by donor and university funding provided resources is about $15,411,000 to $23,116,00 per year (Weisbrod & Weisbrod, 1997).

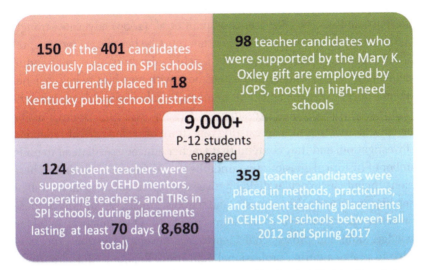

FIGURE 2.2   Teacher education at the CEHD supported by the Mary K. Oxley Foundation

2.2   *An Urgent Look toward the Future in Clinical Teacher Preparation*

Many teacher preparation institutions nationally have generous donors, philanthropy or foundation gifts, or competitive grant funding that can dramatically enhance and improve a program and the preparation of candidates for classrooms. At UofL, the Mary K. Oxley Foundation's generous gift has impacted the preparation of future teachers, the professional growth of classroom teachers, and the academic growth of over 9,000 children since the gift was given. Through this gift and the evolution of a clinical model of educator and teacher preparation, CEHD has been able to further expand its work and impacts with the University's Signature Partnership Initiative to students who experience at-risk circumstances (Bettini & Park, 2017), from four to six partner schools. In 2018–2019, CEHD began developing a new partnership with a seventh prospective SPI-affiliate high school in JCPS, Fairdale High School. Our work with and opportunities to authentically and meaningful engage in these SPI schools is a constant source of inspiration for CEHD faculty, staff, and our candidates in educator preparation programs. As stated in CEHD's original proposal to the Mark K. Oxley Foundation, we are dedicated to the highest levels of learning and the social emotional well-being for all children, individuals, and families, particularly in underserved areas. This is a crucial part of the college's mission in providing ongoing support for access to high-quality teaching and learning for students in the Louisville Metro JCPS schools.

However, as Cochran-Smith et al. (2015) remind teacher educators, there are still urgent reforms to be addressed and a need for research on teacher preparation for the knowledge society and research on teacher preparation for diversity and equity. Likewise, Grossman et al. (2009) advocate strongly that a future direction for teacher education must be based on a reconceptualization of teaching and advocate that teacher educators need to attend to the clinical aspects of practice and experiment with how best to help teacher candidates develop skilled, emergent practice. By taking clinical practice seriously in teacher preparation, Grossman et al. (2015) assert that there must be pedagogies of enactment to an existing repertoire of pedagogies of reflection and investigation, and they contend that teacher educators will need to undo a number of historical divisions that underlie the education of teachers. These divisions include a curricular divide between program coursework as well as the separation between the university and schools. Finally, the authors propose that teacher education be organized around a core set of practices in which knowledge, skill, and professional identity are developed in the process of learning to practice during professional education. Rigorous clinical partnerships between P-12 and higher education should provide authentic laboratory settings for these critical efforts and improved models of practice (Grossman et al., 2015). Advancing teacher preparation through clinical partnerships in the Signature Partnership Initiative schools has allowed us the opportunity to take a very visible and impactful leadership role in addressing these diverse challenges, hopefully in a sustainable and meaningful way for the lives and learning of students, in JCPS schools and our community. We look forward to learning from others and to sharing more in meaningful and dialogic contexts about our changing and evolving teacher preparation programs, delivered through P-12 district and school clinical partnerships.

References

Adams, G., Danielson, C., Moilanen, G., & Association for Supervision and Curriculum Development. (2009). *Enhancing professional practice: A framework for teaching.* Alexandria, VA: ASCD.

Alter, J., & Coggshall, J. G. (2009). *Teaching as a clinical practice profession: Implications for teacher preparation and state policy.* New York, NY: The New York Comprehensive Center and the National Comprehensive Center on Teacher Quality.

American Association of Colleges for Teacher Education (AACTE). (2010). *The clinical preparation of teachers: A policy brief. Teacher preparation: Who needs it? The clinical component.* Washington, DC: National Press Club, March 11, 2018.

American Association of Colleges for Teacher Education (AACTE). (2018). *A pivot toward clinical practice, its lexicon, and the renewal of educator preparation.* Washington, DC: A report of the AACTE Clinical Practice Commission.

Ball, D. L., & Forzani, F. M. (2011). Building a common core for learning to teach and connecting professional learning to practice. *American Educator, 35*(2), 17–21, 38–39.

Bettini, E., & Park, Y. (2017). Novice teachers' experiences in high-poverty schools: An integrative literature review. *Urban Education.* doi:10.1177/0042085916685763

Boyer, E. L. (1990). *Scholarship reconsidered. Priorities of the professoriate* (1st ed., The Carnegie Foundation for the Advancement of Teaching). New York, NY: John Wiley and Sons.

Bronfenbrenner, U., & Morris, P. (1998). The ecology of developmental processes. In R. M. Lerner (Ed.), *Theoretical models of human development* (5th ed., Vol. 1, pp. 993–1028, Handbook of Child Psychology). New York, NY: Wiley.

Cochran-Smith, M., Feiman-Nemser, S., & McIntyre, D. J. (Eds.), & Demers, K. E. (Associate Ed.). (2008). *Handbook of research on teacher education: Enduring questions in changing contexts* (3rd ed.). New York, NY: Routledge, Taylor and Francis Group and the Association of Teacher Educators.

Cochran-Smith, M., Villegas, A. M., Abrams, L., Chavez-Moreno, L., Mills, T., & Stern, R. (2015). Critiquing teacher preparation research. An overview of the field, Part II. *Journal of Teacher Education, 66*(2), 109–121.

Collaboration for Effective Educator Development, Accountability and Reform (CEEDAR). (2018, September 8). Retrieved from http://ceedar.education.ufl.edu

Council for the Accreditation of Educator Preparation. (2018, September 7). *Standard.* Retrieved from http://caepnet.org/standards/standard-2

Cowan, J., & Goldhaber, D. (2015). *National Board Certification: Evidence from Washington State* (CEDR Working Paper 2015-3). Seattle, WA: University of Washington. Retrieved from http://www.cedr.us/papers/working/CEDR%20WP%202015-3_NBPTS%20Cert.pdf

Danielson, C. (2009). *Implementing the framework for teaching in enhancing professional practice.* Alexandria, VA: Association for Supervision and Curriculum Development.

Darling-Hammond, L. (1999). The case for university-based teacher education. In R. Roth (Ed.), *The role of the university in the preparation of teachers* (pp. 19–36). New York, NY: Routledge.

Darling-Hammond, L. (2006). Constructing 21st century teacher education. *Journal of Teacher Education, 57*(3), 300–314.

Darling-Hammond, L. (2006). *Powerful teacher education: Lessons from exemplary programs.* San Francisco, CA: Jossey-Bass.

Grant, C., & Agosto, V. (2008). Teacher capacity and social justice in teacher education. In M. Cochran-Smith, S. Feiman-Nemser, & D. J. McIntyre (Eds.), & K. E. Demers (Associate Ed.), *Handbook of research on teacher education: Enduring questions in changing contexts* (3rd ed.). New York, NY: Routledge, Taylor and Francis Group and the Association of Teacher Educators.

Grossman, P., Mannerness, K., & McDonald, M. (2009). Redefining teaching, re-imaging teacher education. *Teachers and Teaching: Theory and Practice, 12*(2), 273–289.

Kentucky Department of Education. (2018, September 3). *Educator development and equity*. Retrieved from https://education.ky.gov/teachers/Pages/default.aspx

Kentucky Department of Education. (2018, September 8). *Growth and evaluation*. Retrieved from https://education.ky.gov/teachers/PGES/Pages/PGES.aspx

Kentucky Legislative Research Council. (2018, September 3). Retrieved from http://www.lrc.ky.gov/kar/016/002/040.htm

Kentucky Teacher Performance Standards. (2018, September 3). Retrieved from http://www.epsb.ky.gov/mod/book/view.php?id=133

Kini, T., & Podolsky, A. (2016). *Does teaching experience increase teacher effectiveness? A review of the research* (Research brief). Palo Alto, CA: Learning Policy Institute.

Larson, A., & Kyle, D. (Eds.). (2014). Clinical partnerships in teacher education: Perspectives, practices, and outcomes. *Peabody Journal of Education, 89*(4).

McLeskey, J., & Brownell, M. (2015). *High-leverage practices and teacher preparation in special education* (Document No. PR-1). (2018, September 7). University of Florida, Collaboration for Effective Educator Development, Accountability, and Reform Center. Retrieved from http://ceedar.education.ufl.edu/tools/best-practice-review/

National Board for Professional Teaching Standards (NBPTS). (2018, September 7). Retrieved from https://www.nbpts.org

National Council for Accreditation of Teacher Education (NCATE). (2010). *Transforming teacher education through clinical practice: A national strategy to prepare effective teachers*. Report of the Blue Ribbon Panel on clinical preparation and partnerships for improved student learning. Washington, DC.

Nystrand Center of Excellence in Education (NCEE). (2018, September 3). Retrieved from http://louisville.edu/education/centers/nystrand

University of Louisville. (2018, September 7). *Signature partnership*. Retrieved from http://louisville.edu/communityengagement/signature-partnership-1within

University of Louisville, College of Education and Human Development's conceptual framework, Ideas to Action: Shaping Tomorrow. (2018, September 3). Retrieved from http://louisville.edu/education/about/files/conceptual-framework2015.pdf

Weisbrod, G., & Weisbrod, B. (1997). *Measuring economic impacts of projects and programs*. Boston, MA: Economic Development Research Group.

CHAPTER 3

Mentoring and Third Space in the Academy: The Complexities of Community Engaged Scholarship in Clinical Partnerships

Lori Norton-Meier

Abstract

As all the following chapter authors in this text are emerging scholars (at the beginning of their academic careers), in this chapter we hear from an established scholar who has been doing the work of creating and sustaining clinical partnerships for over 20 years. Reflecting on the following chapters and the challenges of not only doing this work but mentoring new scholars and cooperating teachers to be willing to take up this work, Norton-Meier posits that the theorizing around the need to create a "third space" for the children we work with in classrooms also needs to happen for the adults who are working to support the development of new teachers.

Keywords

mentoring – new faculty – teacher education – community engaged scholarship

> I think I will title my first article about our work here, "Winning and losing on Bechum Street." Every day seems like either a "win" (getting into a new classroom, someone making an invitation to join in) or a "loss" (door slammed in my face, unanswered emails, or the forever – not yet – response). I can't help but feel that our location is a huge barrier – that our classroom is located outside the actual school building in a portable classroom trailer adds a complexity that makes us an appendage on Bechum Street that is forgotten until my (university) students walk in the building.
> AN EMAIL TO A COLLEAGUE FROM MY FIRST YEAR AS A COLLEGE PROFESSOR (1998)

∴

1 Introduction

Twenty years ago, I began my career in academia and choosing to work places that were investing in the conceptualization of teaching preservice teachers in actual public school settings. I've worked at four institutions and each one blossomed at a time in educational history when these partnerships located in actual elementary schools were called professional development schools or clinical partnerships. From the few sentences above, it is clear from my first semester as an academic that I was already aware of the messy realities of trying to create, maintain, and sustain these partnerships. As the majority of authors in this text are emerging scholars (at the beginning of their academic careers), in this chapter we hear from an established scholar who posits that the theorizing around the need to create a "third space" for the children we work with in classrooms also needs to happen for the adults who are working to support the development of new teachers. This chapter ends with a discussion of the messy reality of mentoring new scholars in urban clinical partnerships and how to support their emerging community-engaged scholarship.

2 Previous Studies of "Third Space" in the Study of Clinical Partnerships

In 2010, I wrote a chapter with my colleague Dr. Corey Drake focused on our work in understanding the intersection between our mathematics and literacy methods courses that we taught in a local elementary school. We conceptualized the intersection between our two courses for preservice teachers through a theoretical lens of third space thinking. A definition of "third space" provided by Gutierrez and others described third space as "a place where two scripts or two normative patterns of interaction intersect, creating the potential for authentic interaction and learning to occur" (Gutierrez et al., 1997, p. 372). Looking more deeply into our data and what we created, it became clear to us that, while we have in fact created a physical third space, the spaces we are most interested in are both more complex and more abstract than the library. They are spaces of learning, teaching, pushing against boundaries and exchanging resources (Norton-Meier & Drake, 2010).

In considering third space theory in relation to mentoring faculty working in clinical partnership settings, we recognize that two scripts that collide include teaching and scholarship. For every author featured in this text and for many scholars working similarly in Colleges of Education and in the preparation of teachers, they began their professional careers as teachers. Teachers of youth in middle school mathematics. Teachers of 4th grade students. Teachers of English Language learners. Teachers of parents and families. After earning a doctorate, many still argue their strongest identity or script is that of teacher. When their work begins as researchers, scholars, writers of academic prose, and teacher educators, the scripts of their former selves as teachers in K-12 settings bumps up against this new script of being an academic. It is a natural progression that many of these scholars are drawn to the unique settings of clinical partnership models where their two scripts can exist simultaneously in a third space where they are given the opportunity to think and ideate in complex ways about problems of practice, particularly in the preparation of teachers in urban settings.

3 Four Profiles of Scholarly Work in the "Third Space"

Over my twenty-year career in academia, I now find myself in a role of mentoring new scholars into working in clinical partnership settings in elementary schools (preschool-Grade 5). Over time, I have witnessed four unique profiles of how this work is taken up and what I believe creates a unique conversation about how we mentor each of these teacher scholars. Each profile will be discussed in the following paragraphs. Please note, I used pseudonyms for each of the profiles presented here.

3.1 *Deer in the Headlights*

Eleanor approached her time at Bates Elementary Schools with what I call a "deer in the headlights" perspective. If you are not familiar with the term, when a deer sees the headlights of a car, it is known to freeze in place not able to move to get out of the way of the oncoming vehicle. Eleanor found herself suddenly assigned to teach at an elementary school but had no idea where to start, how to begin, or any thoughts about how to adapt her teaching to make the most useful and powerful learning opportunities for her students. The first challenge? Eleanor was assigned to do this—not by choice so her commitment and prior understanding of clinical partnerships was forced and immediate rather than providing her with thoughtful contemplation and choice in this new location and opportunity for not only the preservice teachers but also for the teachers and children in the elementary school.

The first semester, Eleanor simply stayed in the classroom provided at the elementary school. She taught her class as she would on campus with no interaction with anyone outside the University Teacher Learning Lab classroom at Bates Elementary. In this case, it was the Teacher in Residence (TiR) that made the first invitation to Eleanor to ask her students to participate in the Family night being held at the school. That invitation and participation nudged Eleanor to see the first point of collaboration, assisting with Family Night and giving her students leadership roles to work with a teacher to run various activities for children and families. The confidence grew and Eleanor created an afterschool and summer reading program. Once again, this was structured to include preservice teacher education students as tutors giving them the opportunity to practice various reading methods they had learned in class and support young readers.

3.2   *Window Shopping*

Ariel excitedly embraced the opportunity to teach at Dedham Elementary School. An award-winning elementary teacher herself, she believed she was at her best in the company of children. Yet, when she arrived at the school, she couldn't find a teacher willing to give up classroom time to have Ariel come in to do model teaching, have her students teach small groups of children, or even work individually with children during reader's workshop time. Working with the Teacher-in-Residence (TiR), Ariel asked the teachers if they could come in while the children were away at special area (art, music, physical education, library time) so that the students could look at the empty elementary classroom to visualize how a teacher sets up a classroom to maximize literacy instruction. All teachers agreed and much to Ariel's delight, each teacher stayed in his or her empty classroom and would explain how the class was arranged, how children interacted in the space, and answered questions from the preservice teachers.

When the tour of empty classrooms concluded, Ariel had read about a project called "Instructional Rounds" (City et al., 2009) and she asked the teachers if she could bring her students through in groups of 2–3 and they would spend 15 minutes observing literacy instruction, step into the hallway for a 10-minute de-brief, and then move on to another classroom. This way the students were able to see five different grade levels and think about literacy instruction adjusts for each developmental level of elementary-aged student. The de-brief time also became a time that the administrators in the building, the reading specialists, and educational associates would join our preservice teachers in the hallway to assist in the de-brief in an effort to help them connect teaching and learning to theory, research, and practice.

3.3   *Partner in Practice*

Fatima requested to be at Nelson Elementary School particularly because of her interest in working with English Language Learners (ELs). Her own dissertation was centered around working with two third grade teachers and her ultimate goal was to start a new research study while growing her teaching identity by exposing her mathematics students to teaching practices to use with children who spoke a variety of languages.

During the summer before she would teacher her first class at the elementary school, she met with the principal to identify one or possibly two teachers that would potentially be good partners to begin this collaborative endeavor. The principal enthusiastically recommended three 1st grade teachers who had two, six, and 12 years of experience teaching ELs. Fatima met regularly with the teachers to plan unique experiences that would benefit both the preservice teachers and the 1st grade children. Demonstration teaching by Fatima was welcomed and became a peer observation tool for the 1st grade teachers that fueled their own discussion about teaching practices and student learning. The biggest frustration is that many more teachers in the school building wanted to be involved in working with Fatima and have the preservice teachers in their classrooms. One way Fatima helped bridge the desire of more teachers wanting to be involved was to create the "Pen Pal Project" where third grade students wrote letters weekly to a preservice teacher education student including a math problem to try to stump the pen pal. The PST would write back answering the math problem while including a problem of their own. Not only did the PSTs learn about children's approaches to mathematical problem solving but they could also analyze and support the writing of this group of students who were also ELs.

3.4   *Schoolwide Playtime*

Tanya was re-assigned from another elementary school to build a new partnership with a local elementary school at the principal's request. The school was close to the university and offered an opportunity of proximity that would allow students easy access to campus by walking or biking. In addition, the teachers in the school were eager to participate—not just one or two—but every teacher. Yet, Tanya asked the question about how this could be done with one small group of literacy methods students (approximately 19 college students). With the TiR, they created an immediate strategy called the "Breakfast Brigade." At this school, all students ate breakfast in the classroom so it created a time in the morning where the preservice teachers could go in pairs and read to children while they ate breakfast. It gave Tanya's students the opportunity to practice the art of the read aloud while learning to ask deep questions, engage in prereading strategies that would help children use their prior knowledge to connect to the text, and to focus on what they were learning about how readers comprehend texts. This morning strategy began to build the trust and relationships necessary to build the solid foundation for deeper future collaborations including a writer's workshop where each student created a digital story with a preservice teacher writing buddy.

3.5 De-Briefing the Four Profiles

What is it that opens and creates these third spaces for teacher-researcher-scholars who take up work in clinical partnership elementary school settings? In the previous four profiles, key elements are revealed: (1) Proximity, (2) Time, and (3) Teacher Scholar as Decision Maker.

3.5.1 Proximity

Space matters. Location matters. It may seem trivial to begin the discussion of "third space" theory and thinking with a focus on actual space but each of these four profiles indicate that if the teacher scholar only sees the learning environment as the one classroom in the elementary school that is assigned, we would have to question if any third space (as it is theoretically conceptualized) is occurring or can occur. If the college classroom is simply moved to the elementary space and the way we teach is not re-constructed or negotiated in new ways with the entirety of the practices that happen within the school, then third space simply becomes a third space to continue the status quo whereas third space as a theoretical construct argues that this is a space where new thinking is generated, new scripts emerge, and old ways of knowing can be challenged.

3.5.2 Time

When examining the four profiles, each partnership took time. Time to develop relationships. Time to build trust and an understanding of who the people are in the school – children, families, teachers, administration. Time for the teacher scholar to wrestle with who they have been as a teacher and how they need to think differently in this new space, with new collaborators, and in considering their content area as well as the expectations from the profession and for teacher certification. Relationships are critical in third space theorizing and this cannot happen without shared power and trust.

3.5.3 Teacher Scholar as Decision-Maker

The decision to be in this space must be owned by the teacher scholar. In the first profile, Eleanor was assigned to this space making it difficult for her to conceptualize how her work would be different from how she traditionally taught in an on-campus learning space. With each profile, the teacher scholar demonstrated a path of "becoming" in the third space where each could make decisions about how to bring together the scripts of "teacher" and "scholar" allowing them to collide in the third space to be negotiated, analyzed, revised, and presented in a continual act of re-defining what it means to learn to be a teacher. This path will not be the same for each teacher scholar so the support of their own decision-making at each stage of their development needs support to help them as they grow in new areas of "community engaged scholarship" (Boyer, 1990).

4 Recognizing the Complexities of Community Engaged Scholarship in Schools

> In *Scholarship Reconsidered,* the late Ernest Boyer contends that in addition to valuing the generation of knowledge (the traditional definition of scholarship), higher education should also support the application of knowledge through faculty engagement in community-based research, teaching and service (Boyer, 1990). Community-engaged scholarship can apply to teaching (e.g. service-learning, research (e.g. community-based participatory research), and service (e.g. community service, outreach, advocacy). (From the University of Louisville website, 2018)

How can faculty ensure that their community-engaged teaching, scholarship, and research supports successful promotion and tenure? The above statement shows the ideological support from our own institution and a call for changing a traditional definition of scholarship. Historically, academia identifies published professional articles (research and non-research), books, and book chapters as acceptable products that support tenure and promotion. Community-engaged work in schools can result in these products, as well as non-traditional products such as curriculum products, technical reports, videos, artistic productions and community-focused literature.

What advice can be offered to the teacher scholar who is attempting to build a systemic understanding of the power of this line of work and the need for it in the profession? The following six strategies offer the start to an action plan in institutions of higher education:

- Engage the conversation. With individuals, in groups, across departments and colleges, it is critical to engage the conversation. Include personnel committees who make decisions about tenure and promotion so that the conversation can begin to negotiate what a dossier might look like from teacher scholars who are expected to take up this work in clinical partnership sites particularly K-12 school settings where powerful teaching, research, and scholarship can emerge and impact the preparation of teachers.
- Show, don't tell. It is critical to showcase the clinical partnership sites. To create the best understanding, administrators and policy makers need to

see the power of the work in action. Don't just tell about the wonderful things that are happening in these spaces. Talk about the complexities of doing this work and show how working in such spaces in all the complexities assists in supporting new teachers to understand the lives of teachers in schools.
- Consider new impact metrics. How do we show the impact of our work? Where could we demonstrate the power of this work with different types of metrics?
- Research and Theorize. Central to the work that we do is to theorize teaching and learning. If we change the way we do our work—in clinical partnership settings—perhaps we also need to think of new research methodologies to examine and explore teaching and learning—for children, preservice teachers, families, educators, and administrators in these spaces.
- Make no apologies. I end with a bit of personal-professional advice. Too often I hear my mentees apologize for this work. Unique work that doesn't follow traditional patterns of what counts as teaching, research, and service. I reiterate "make no apologies" for this work that is incredibly complex, challenging to a status quo view of many problems of practice, and the space where many of us find a place where we allow two scripts to collide—that of teacher and that of scholar—providing a unique space of thinking to understand these problems of practice in new ways.

References

Boyer, E. (1990). *Scholarship reconsidered: Priorities of the professoriate.* Princeton, NJ: Carnegie Foundation for the Advancement of Teaching.

City, E. A., Elmore, R. F., Furman, R. F., & Teitel, L. (2009). *Instructional rounds in education: A network approach to improving teaching and learning.* Cambridge, MA: Harvard Education Press.

Gutierrez, K., Baquedano-Lopez, P., & Turner, M. G. (1997). Putting language back into language arts: When the radical middle meets the third space. *Language Arts, 74*(5), 368–378.

Norton-Meier, L., & Drake, C. (2010). When third space is more than the library: The complexities of theorizing and learning to use family and community resources to teach elementary literacy and mathematics. In V. Ellis, A. Edwards, & P. Smagorinsky (Eds.), *Cultural-historical perspectives on teacher education and development* (pp. 196–211). London: Routledge.

University of Louisville. (2018). *Community partnerships for teaching, research and service.* Retrieved October 20, 2018, from https://louisville.edu/facultyhandbook/teaching-research-and-service-resources

CHAPTER 4

Navigating Synergic Boundaries: A Collaboration between an Urban Elementary School and a School-Based Mathematics Methods Course

Lateefah Id-Deen, Gabrielle Read-Jasnoff, Shannon Putman and Tim Foster

Abstract

Teaching itself has changed, as has the context within which teaching occurs, so it is crucial that strong university-school partnerships are established (Le Cornu, 2010; Martin, Snow, & Torrez, 2011). Clinical models promise to be an effective way to prepare teachers because they directly connect teacher education programs to teaching practice (Darling-Hammond, Hammerness, Grossman, Rust, & Shulman, 2003). The chapter examines the ways a mathematics teacher educator worked collaboratively with urban elementary teachers, administrators and school personnel. More specifically, we describe how the mathematics teacher educator was responsive to the context by focusing on equitable instructional practices and the importance of mathematics fluency. We show how this partnership works to supports prospective elementary teachers' journey as they learn to teach mathematics. Recommendations for (mathematics) teacher educators and school administrators who plan to implement school-based methods courses will be discussed.

Keywords

clinical partnership – methods course – preservice teacher perspectives

1   Overview

University-school partnerships can be an effective way to prepare teachers because they directly connect teacher education programs to teaching practice (Darling-Hammond, Hammerness, Grossman, Rust, & Shulman, 2003). The chapter examines the ways a mathematics teacher educator worked collaboratively with urban elementary teachers, administrators and school personnel at a professional development school (PDS). More specifically, we hone in on one concept, mathematics fluency, and describe how a mathematics teacher educator was responsive to an urban elementary school by incorporating a variety of strategies emphasizing that concept in a school-based mathematics methods course to support equitable instructional practices in K-6 classrooms. Although the instructional approaches of the school and mathematics teacher educator were different, both methods kept improving students' understanding of mathematics and supporting prospective elementary teachers at the forefront. Recommendations for mathematics teacher educators, school personnel, and researchers who plan to implement school-based methods courses will be discussed.

2   Introduction

Professional development schools (PDSs) can be an effective way to prepare teachers because they directly connect teacher education programs to current teaching practices (Darling-Hammond, Hammerness, Grossman, Rust, & Shulman, 2003). In PDSs, prospective teachers have an opportunity to learn theory in their university classroom and have chances to practice and/or observe strategies that connect to theory in schools. Research on partnerships among universities and K-12 school education reforms has existed in the United States for over twenty years (Carnegie Forum, 1986; Callahan & Martin, 2007; Holmes Group, 1986; Kennedy, 1992; Levine, 1992). However, when university-school partnerships enact, the power differential favors the university faculty member (Hooper & Britnell, 2012; Trent & Lim, 2010). To alleviate this concern, the authors worked closely with one another to be intentional about working with teachers to learn ways to discuss some of the instructional strategies used in the K-6 mathematics classrooms. Through this partnership, PSTs (preservice teachers) were able to witness different instructional approaches where the ultimate goal is to improve elementary students' mathematics fluency.

Cochran Elementary School has an emphasis on supporting their students' fluency in mathematics. This chapter examines the ways a mathematics teacher educator was responsive to an urban elementary school by incorporating a greater emphasis on mathematics fluency in a mathematics methods course to support equitable instructional practices in K-6 classrooms. Collaboration between the school and university was vital in order to support the PSTs at the school.

This chapter does not highlight a research study, instead we focus on showcasing the ways a mathematics teacher educator collaborated with school personnel to support PSTs as they learned various instructional strategies to teach mathematics. Additionally, we highlight reflections from PSTs about their experiences as it pertains to learning about mathematics fluency. First, we detail research-based strategies for mathematics fluency used at Cochran Elementary School and the mathematics methods course taught at the school. Then, we describe the context of both settings. Next, we showcase some PSTs reflections of their perceptions of learning about two research-based strategies for mathematics fluency. Finally, we conclude the chapter by discussing recommendations for mathematics teacher educators, school personnel, and researchers who plan to implement school-based methods courses in K-12 schools in order to build an effective university-school partnership.

3 Research-Based Strategies for Mathematics Fluency

Procedural fluency is "skill in carrying out procedures flexibly, accurately, efficiently, and appropriately" (CCSSO, 2010; NCTM 2014; NRC, 2001). Early mathematical fluency, as explained by Baroody (2006), includes single-digit addition, multiplication, subtraction, and division. Children navigate through counting strategies, reasoning, and mastery to become mathematically fluent. The first phase involves physical or verbal counting to derive solutions. The second stage uses previous knowledge as a deductive technique to answer new/unknown expertise. The third and final phase occurs when efficient (of quickness and ease) answers are produced. Children can navigate these three steps, as described by Baroody (2006), using conventional wisdom or the number-sense view. Cochran teachers and administrators advocate for more traditional knowledge, which they refer to as reflex math. Conversely, university faculty advocate for a number-sense perspective on how fluency arrives. We further discuss each strategy, specific to their three stages, below.

Conventional wisdom emphasizes that mastery can be achieved without phases one and two of the process. Fact recall, or the "automatic retrieval of the associated answer to an expression," Ex. $9 \times 2 = 18$ can represent fluency. Mastery develops as children memorize individual facts using rote repeated practices and reinforcements. Additionally, a well-designed drill is thought to be the best way to help students arrive at mastery. Learning difficulties are typically a result of defects specific to the learner. Unfortunately, students who encounter such difficulties likely get stuck in the first phase of computation development. Only recognizable and replicable reasoning strategies can help students' progress into phase two, though it may be only temporary. However, many never reach the third phase. Conversely, in a number sense view, phases one and two are essential. It is in these phases "mastery that underlies computational fluency grows out of discovering the numerous patterns and relationships that interconnect the basic combinations" (Baroody, 2006, p. 24). In phases one and two, students build their conceptual understandings through the discovery of patterns and relationships. Here, reasoning strategies develop that establish computational fluency in stage three. Learning difficulties from a number-sense view are typically the results of defects in conventional instructional practices. Mastery achievement occurs without purposeful, meaningful, inquiry-based instruction that promotes number sense.

The three crucial phases of the number-sense view are but one critical step in the five fundamentals of fact fluency (Bay-Williams & King, in press). First, mastery must focus on fluency. The learner should understand the meaning of the expression, not just its solution. Second are the three developmental phases. As described above, students should sequentially progress through counting, reasoning, and then mastery. Third, knowing foundational facts must precede derived facts. Using knowledge such as total of 10 can help students understand 6 + 7 (Ex. 6 + 4 = 10. 4 is 3 less than 7, so 6 + 7 = 10 + 3, 13). Fourth, students need to provide substantial and enjoyable practice. Practice should be rigorous and applicable to their everyday lives. And fifth, fluency cannot be assessed with timed tests. We further describe specifics to how these five fundamentals of fact fluency are evident in this particular school-university partnership in detail by the university instructor below.

4   Cochran Elementary School

This chapter focuses specifically on the "boundary crossing," as described by Engestrom et al. (1995), between a college of education and an urban elementary school, which is a space that connects theory to practice. Cochran Elementary is an example of what Lieberman and Miller (1990) claim as a professional practice school. Cochran operates based on public school governance instead of university lab schools, which are typically independent of school boards, etc. A priority in this school is supporting students' fact fluency.

Students with fact-fluency deficits in early elementary school who do not receive specific interventions fail to catch up with their peers in later elementary school (Chong & Siegel, 2008). These computational fluency deficits compound difficulties as the math curriculum become more complicated (Geary, 2004). Research conducted by Chong, Siegel, and others led the principal of Cochran Elementary, Tim Foster, to create a school-wide culture to support mathematics fluency. When Principal Foster took over, Cochran Elementary ranked the second to last performing elementary school in the state of

Kentucky. Four years later, through hard work from all stakeholders, Cochran Elementary is now rated as a proficient school. The primary area that Principal Foster and the staff decided to focus on was mathematics fluency. Through multiple research-based programs, interventions, and countless time spent, Cochran students outperformed their peers in state testing. The state average for African American boys in the area of math growth for the 2016–2017 state testing was 60%. African American boys at Cochran Elementary scored 76% growth in mathematics.

This success did not come just from the increased use of flash cards, but rather an entire school that was focused and driven to improve each child's mathematics fluency. Any adult staff member at Cochran will ask a student, from any grade, a mathematics fluency question as they pass them in the hall. There are mathematics fluency facts posted all over the building for students to practice as they wait for the restroom or to go to their locker. Every year Cochran holds a mathematics bee that is one of the most significant events at the school. Students are required to spend 20 minutes on a mathematics fluency, computer-based intervention program daily. This program has a game-like approach, so students will choose to spend their extra time playing. They also have reached out to the community by providing resources such as tablets to parents so students can work on this program at home. Cochran changed the culture of its school, it started with Principal Foster, and the results have been seen in multiple areas, including but not limited to state testing.

5   School-Based Elementary Mathematics Methods Course

The umbrella of school-university partnerships can look very different. Some focus more heavily on student-teacher observations and clinical placements, while others emphasize instructor-led teacher education coursework. While engaged in coursework, prospective elementary teachers and their university instructor observe mathematics taught by practicing teachers. Debriefing of theory and practice usually follow the classroom observations in the methods course. Zeichner (2010) describes a partnership, known as mediated instruction and field experiences, which aligns with the school-based methods course. The mathematics methods course meets once weekly at the school to observe teachers using pedagogical practices similar or different from strategies discussed in the methods course. Further, the schools' personnel, Teacher in Residence (TiR), works with the methods instructor, connecting course objectives to be observed by school staff. Before the school-based elementary mathematics methods course was taught, the instructor had multiple conversations about mathematics initiatives that occur in the school. As a result of multiple conversations there is a greater emphasis on mathematics fluency in the course to support PSTs as they develop understandings of mathematical ideas children construct in their mathematics classroom. They also become familiar with, evaluate, and implement instructional techniques, materials, technologies, and methods that facilitate all children's mathematical learning based on best practice research. The course examines five key areas: culturally responsive mathematics pedagogy, mathematical content, curriculum, attitudes, and collaboration. They also explore research-based "teaching and learning" best practices that are relevant for facilitating equitable mathematics learning experiences for all learners.

In the school-based methods course, we define fluency, because there are a variety of interpretations for procedural fluency, more generally (Kling & Bay-Williams, 2014). We focus on basic fact fluency, which Baroody (2006) describes as "the efficient, appropriate, and flexible application of single-digit calculation skills and ... an essential aspect of mathematical proficiency" (p. 22). To support this, we focus on understanding student thinking as it relates to counting strategies and reasoning to become mathematically fluent. For example, a robust approach, number talks, helps students develop fluency and flexible thinking in the classroom (Parrish, 2010). For this particular strategy, we discuss concepts in class through readings, videos and engaging in number talks. Throughout the semester, we discuss the various strategies for students learning mathematics fluency. We engage in conversations about students memorizing facts before learning strategies and vice versa. Although we do not address each approach in-depth, they can compare their experiences of learning about teaching fluency to the ways students learn mathematics fluency. Because we cannot review every strategy in the course, it is helpful for students to witness different approaches during their observations that occur outside of the school-based methods course at Cochran Elementary. The overall goal is to make connections between academic and practitioner knowledge supporting appropriate pedagogical practices is an utmost priority.

6   Preservice Teachers' Persepectives on Their Experiences

There were 15 PSTs in the school-based mathematics methods course. During their time in the course, the PSTs witnessed various approaches to supporting students as they become fluent in mathematics. In this section, we share some written reflections from PSTs about their experiences as it relates to observing practices that support mathematics fluency for students. Overall, the PSTs really enjoyed seeing different types of strategies and having an opportunity to discuss their observations in the school-based mathematics methods course. One student noted,

> In our classes we normally learn something completely different from what we see in the classrooms. I loved being able to ask questions [about] what we saw in the classroom. It was also helpful that you [instructor] knew what we were asking about.

Oftentimes there are disconnects between what students see in the classrooms and learn in their courses. Because the instructor and school personnel worked together, the instructor anticipated some of the misalignments. Another student was relieved she did not have to 'choose' one way. She noted, "Many times we leave our classes feeling like we have to choose which way to teach, but I learned that there are multiple ways to teach mathematics fluency." Another student discussed the disconnect between theory and practice. She stated,

> I wish professors would just understand that things in our classes and in schools are done differently. At Cochran, students have to pass state tests, which is why they use certain strategies. As much as we want to wait forever for students to understand material that is not realistic. In class, we're able to talk about those issues and really understand what was going on in the school and why.

This student appreciated the conversations the instructor was able to have with them. The instructor was able to articulate the reasons behind practices because she was closely connected to school personnel. Another student appreciated the extra time spent on mathematics fluency in the class. She stated,

> The minute you walk in the school, you see posters and banners showing the importance of fluency. You see teachers stopping kids in the hallways to ask their facts. It's a big part of the school. I appreciated us spending more time on fluency in class, so we can know the different ways to teach fluency.

This statement really speaks to the appreciation for the emphasis of fluency in the course in order to align with the goals of the school. Collaboration was crucial as the TiR and mathematics teacher educator worked towards providing worthwhile learning experiences for the PSTs.

7   Collaboration Is Essential

Though school-university partnerships can provide significant benefits for all parties involved, establishing and maintaining a successful relationship is not always easy (Bartholomew & Sandholtz, 2009; Id-Deen, Mark, & Thomas, 2019). Foundational conditions include time management, relationships and roles based on trust, and ownership and accountability. Fundamental shifts and changes in structure, purpose, and relation are also necessary (Baumfield & Butterworth, 2007). As Bartholomew and Sandholtz (2009) found, initially partnerships may have collective goals, but non-parallel goals may arise and can potentially compromise work. District administration sometimes view teachers as implementers of curriculum, while university instructors advocate for teachers to promote comprehensive expertise. Unfortunately, state and district testing and accountability can create a context where policy and instructional practice can be difficult terrain to navigate. Specifically, in the partnership between the University of Louisville and Cochran Elementary, procedural fluency and its recommended instruction can look very different.

Although school-university partnerships can be challenging, collaboration is key to any PDS model (Ball & Rundquist, 1993; Cozza, 2010; Grisham et al., 2002; Lieberman, 1995; Taymans et al., 2012; Trachtman, 2007). The school and university represent a cyclic relationship, as the products of one are the incoming population of the other (Clark, 1999). Both teachers and university faculty take on shared responsibility for the development of preservice teacher candidates. The active collaboration includes both teachers and university faculty improvement in a myriad of ways. This relationship, above almost all others, can be the key to an effective semester for all members of the professional development team. This alliance takes a delicate balance that demands full investment from all members into the process.

Cochran Elementary has a designated person that works as the mediator between the university-based math educator and the school-based teacher. This TiR is set up to create fluid and highly useful collaboration experiences. According to Doolittle (2008), building a successful school and university partnership requires time upfront to establish ground rules, clarify the tasks to be undertaken, identify supports as are necessary for successful implementation, and ensure that a shared vision and mission exist between partners. The TiR works directly with the university-based faculty before the semester even commences. Through multiple conversations, they discuss in detail what the university professor wants to accomplish throughout the semester. The professor shares what specific areas she wants her students to experience via observation in a live and engaging classroom. The TiR has the unique knowledge of understanding each teacher's strengths and specific areas that their instruction excels. Together the two discuss, in detail, what teacher would provide the most efficient experience for preservice teachers to observe.

These collaborative conversations are the first and potentially most vital step in creating an authentic culture of learning. The next crucial, yet frequently overlooked step taken by the TiR is to meet with school-based teachers. Without diplomacy during this phase, the results tend toward a negative impression of the collaboration process, leading to a negative culture surrounding the partnership. The TiR must meet with each teacher individually, at a time that is convenient for that teacher. There indeed is an art form to the collaboration process, and the TiR must learn what each teacher needs to hear to buy into the entire process. This buy-in does not happen organically; there needs to be an effort and apparent dedication to this step of the process. Teachers are often told as a whole that they "have" to do many things—whether it is changing standards, new approaches to instruction, or how long they are required to teach certain subjects. They simply do not want another thing they are required to do. If the TiR says, "you are going to do this, and you have no choice," the respect for a culture of open and meaningful collaboration is gone.

Teachers are very protective of their planning time as well. They have very few minutes during the day when they can plan, or just have a break. This time is crucial for their instruction, as well as their mental well-being. To ask a teacher to give up that time can be a difficult demand requiring preliminary thought and planning. The TiR must find the best possible time to meet with that teacher to ensure their mindset is positive to begin. Once the school-based teacher is aware of the process, the TiR then gets to work. The TiR has to efficiently and precisely convey what the university professor requires from them. The TiR explains how many people will be coming into their classroom, what they will be looking at, how long they will stay, what time, among multiple other requests from the professor. The key is to make sure the teacher is not overwhelmed and feels like they have a say in what occurs in their classroom. The collaboration that happens between the TiR and the teacher is a fluid conversation that allows the teacher to have ownership, while still accomplishing the goals stated by the mathematics teacher educator. Without this intricate planning and alliance, condemned collaboration is imminent.

Conversations also occur between the teachers and university faculty member. Together we discuss the theory and concepts to be further explored in the mathematics methods course. This information is relevant because the teacher can make connections between what is done in the classroom and what prospective teachers will learn in the mathematics methods course. For example, earlier in the chapter we stated the mathematics methods course focuses on number talks as a strategy to improve students' mathematics fluency. The mathematics teacher educator talks with the school teacher about the ways to implement number talks in the classroom and how the concepts appears in the mathematics methods course. Therefore, when prospective teachers observe the classroom, they see direct connections between theory/strategies and practice. Creating sustainable and significant internal collaboration requires etching it into the culture of the organization (Dehmlow, 2017). The conversations between the TiR, school teachers, and mathematics teacher educator are integral to ensure worthwhile experiences for prospective teachers.

8 Concluding Thoughts and Recommendations

The need for an improved cohesiveness between teacher practice and education has resulted in the establishment of school-university partnerships (Zimpher & Howey, 2005; Goodlad, 1993). There is an abundance of moving parts that work together to create an effective Professional Development School. The university-based faculty is coming into a potentially unknown environment and trying to integrate not only themselves, but their practices into an already established system. School-based personnel are asked to open their classrooms to professors and PSTs. They are asked to welcome these possible distractions with open arms, knowing it will cause more work for them. The administration has to worry about an increased number of unknown people in their building and the safety concerns that come along with that. Educational focus currently demands schools and their students perform high on standardized tests; to meet these requirements teachers need to teach. Teachers dedicate every possible moment to focused, specific instruction. When method students and professors ask to take some of that instructional time, the payoff must be worthwhile. When all members perform their roles, it not only becomes worth it for all parties involved but provides benefits that non-professional development schools never get to experience. Below are some recommendations for mathematics teacher educators, teachers, administrators, TiRs and researchers who can work towards avoiding the messiness of this process:

Mathematics Teacher Educators:
– Gain an understanding of what is already occurring in the school! Most schools have initiatives, and more important, priorities that they use to support students' mathematics understanding. Consider ways to incorporate those in the mathematics methods course.

- Communicate with school personnel, teachers and administrators! The TiR knows the school, the teachers' strengths and weaknesses, and their job is to support the teacher educator and PSTs' learning experiences. They can schedule observations, obtain needed materials, and handle all the school-based tasks while the faculty member is not on site. This step is crucial when arranging classroom observations of mathematics instruction.
- If the school is not fortunate enough to have a TiR, reach out to other school-based teachers. Get to know them, learn what they feel their strengths and weaknesses are! Let them know that you are not there to interrupt their class. Additionally, reassure the teachers that the classroom observations are not evaluative. Make sure they always feel like they are in control; it is their classroom, and they should have the final say on what happens in it. By letting them maintain this power, they will be more open to suggestions and willing to help.

School-Based Teachers:
- Maintain an open mind! Teachers become teachers because they want to educate. They want to pass knowledge onto others and help them create a better life for themselves. What better way to do that than to educate future educators? Working in a PDS school provides teachers a unique experience to take knowledge that they have gleaned from years of experience, struggles, and perseverance, and pass that on to young teachers who are just starting their journeys. They can tell PSTs all the things they wish someone had told them. Teachers can affect countless students; their skills and knowledge can reach kids far beyond their classroom.
- Be Flexible! Flexibility can be one of the hardest things to ask a classroom teacher to do. They have their routines and schedules planned out to the second, and they do not like disruptions to that. However, the more flexible you can be, the more benefits you will experience. Having a methods student in your classroom can be helpful in ways you never even considered. They can help with behavior, run small groups, perform tasks you may need, and create bonds with students that make everyone better. They are currently learning the newest research and education trends; they might know a strategy that you had never even heard of. Put your pride aside and be willing to listen to what they have to offer.

School Administrators:
- Be Visible! The most important thing for the college students to see is you. You are the leaders of the school, you set the tone and create the entire school culture. Make sure they notice you involved in the classrooms,

showing them how an efficient administrator looks. Stop by their classes and talk with them; let them know what skills you are looking for when you hire a teacher. Help to prepare them for the challenges they face when they try to obtain a job.
– Get them involved! If you have school functions such as a literacy night, ask them to help. Give them the responsibility of planning a school-wide event, so they have that real-world knowledge. Allow them the experience so they can feel what it is like and the real workload.

Teacher in Residence:
– Be Active! It truly is your responsibility to make this work! Your sole job is to make sure that university faculty has what they need. It is your responsibility to find out what the professors want to teach, what they will need from the school, how many students do they need to place, etc. Once you know their needs, you need to figure out the most efficient way to make their goals for the semester a reality.
– Get Moving! Once you know what the university professors need, do it. Meet with teachers, take as little of their time as possible, but meet with them. Find out what days and times work for them. Make sure you reassure them that this will be a benefit not only the PSTs, but them and their students as well. Get them excited about the partnership and convince them to buy into the culture of collaboration.
– Be Available! There is no way possible to list all the things that will be needed. Random problems and issues arise every day. It could be a broken Smart Board, a missing book, or trouble with parking. Make sure everyone knows how to get in touch with you and be proactive. When a class is taking place, be visible. Let the professor know where you are, so if they need you they can reach you. Any interruption to the educational process creates a reason for the stakeholders to withdraw from the collaboration.

Researchers:
– Continuing professional development (CPD) continues to outweigh initial teacher education (ITE) in regards to the majority of school-university partnerships research. As universities and colleges of education embrace ITE partnerships, the authors of this chapter urge faculty to publish their findings and experiences to improve the other school-university partnerships. As research on ITE partnerships progress, Burton and Greher (2007) recommend inclusion of rural, suburban, as well as urban schools. Including, but not limited to, how the collaboration develops, the quality of the process,

the outcomes of the process, and perspectives from all key stakeholders (preservice teachers, in-service teachers, and higher education faculty). Specifically, they address research needs specific to each stakeholder as well as the collaboration itself.

In conclusion, Peters (2002) reminds us that the effects of quality partnerships may become more visible in the long term, versus immediate evidential impact. As the cycle of boundary navigation continues, each institution further develops the driving population of their counterpart. A professional development school is not a simple concept. There are multiple players involved in the process, and it requires complete and total buy-in from all of them. Even though the process can seem challenging at times, the benefits far outweigh the tensions. It provides prospective teachers an opportunity to learn in real schools, where they see the everyday life that they are striving to reach. University professors can maintain relationships, and they too benefit from teaching in an active school environment. They get to watch the practices they are teaching and observe first hand if they are useful. School-based teachers are exposed to the newest methods and also provided extra help in their classroom. The Professional Development School model, when performed correctly, creates opportunities for all, and the most significant benefit goes to the group who need it the most, the prospective teachers.

References

Ball, D. L., & Rundquist, S. S. (1993). Collaboration as context for joining teacher learning with learning about teaching. In D. Cohen, M. McLaughlin, & J. Talbert (Eds.), *Teaching for understanding: Challenges for policy and practice* (pp. 13–42). San Francisco CA: Jossey Bass.

Baroody, A. J. (2006). Why children have difficulties mastering the basic number facts and how to help them. *Teaching Children Mathematics, 13*, 22–31.

Bartholomew, S. S., & Sandholtz, J. H. (2009). Competing views of teaching in a school–university partnership. *Teaching and Teacher Education, 25*(1), 155–165.

Baumfield, V., & Butterworth, M. (2007). Creating and translating knowledge about teaching and learning in collaborative school–university research partnerships: An analysis of what is exchanged across the partnerships, by whom and how. *Teachers and Teaching: Theory and Practice, 13*(4), 411–427.

Burton, S. L., & Greher, G. R. (2007). School–university partnerships: What do we know and why do they matter? *Arts Education Policy Review, 109*(1), 13–24.

Callahan, J. L., & Martin, D. (2007). The spectrum of school–university partnerships: A typology of organizational learning systems. *Teaching and Teacher Education, 23*(2), 136–145.

Carnegie Forum on Education, & the Economy. Task Force on Teaching as a Profession. (1986). *A Nation prepared: Teachers for the 21st century: the report of the task force on teaching as a profession, carnegie forum on education and the economy, May 1986.* Carnegie Forum on Education.

Chong, S. L., & Siegel, L. S. (2008). Stability of computational deficits in math learning disability from second through fifth grades. *Developmental Neuropsychology, 33*(3), 300–317.

Clark, R. W. (1999). School–university partnerships and professional development schools. *Peabody Journal of Education, 74*(3–4), 164–177.

Cozza, B. (2010). Transforming teaching into a collaborative culture: An attempt to create a professional development school-university partnership. *The Educational Forum, 74*(3), 227–241.

Darling-Hammond, L., Hammerness, K., Grossman, P., Rust, F., & Shulman, L. (2005). The design of teacher education programs. In L. Darling-Hammond, J. Bransford, P. LePage, K. Hammerness, & H. Duffy (Eds.), *Preparing teachers for a changing world: What teachers should learn and be able to do* (pp. 390–441). San Francisco, CA: Jossey-Bass.

Engestrom, Y., Engestrom, R., & Karkkainen, M. (1995). Polycontextuality and boundary crossing in expert cognition: Learning and problem solving in complex work activities. *Learning and Instruction, 5*(4), 319–336.

Geary, D. C. (2004). Mathematics and learning disabilities. *Journal of Learning Disabilities, 37*(1), 4–15.

Goodlad, J. I. (1993). School-university partnerships and partner schools. *Educational Policy, 7*(1), 24–39.

Grisham, D. L., Berg, M., Jacobs, V. R., & Mathison, C. (2002). Can a professional development school have a lasting impact on teachers' beliefs and practices? *Teacher Education Quarterly, 29*(3), 7–24.

Holmes Group. (1986). *Tomorrow's teachers.* East Lansing, MI: Holmes Group.

Hooper, L. M., & Britnell, H. B. (2012). Mental health research in K–12 schools: Translating a systems approach to university–school partnerships. *Journal of Counseling & Development, 90*(1), 81–90.

Id-Deen, L., Mark, S., & Thomas, S. (2019). *"Walking on eggshells": Building authentic and trusting relationships between a university and high school clinical model,* submitted.

Kennedy, M. (1992). Establishing professional schools for teachers. In M. Levine (Ed.), *Professional practice schools: Linking teacher education and school reform* (pp. 63–80). New York, NY: Teacher College Press.

Kling, G., & Bay-Williams, J. M. (2014). Assessing basic fact fluency. *Teaching Children Mathematics, 20*(8), 488–497.

Levine, M. (1992). A conceptual framework for professional practice schools. In M. Levine (Ed.), *Professional practice schools: Linking teacher education and school reform* (pp. 8–24). New York, NY: Teacher College Press.

Lieberman, A. (1995). Practices that support teacher development. *Phi Delta Kappan, 76*(8), 591.

Lieberman, A., & Miller, L. (1990). Teacher development in professional practice schools. *Teachers College Record, 92*(1), 105–122.

National Council of Teachers of Mathematics. (2014). *Principles and standards for school mathematics.*

National Research Council, & Mathematics Learning Study Committee. (2001). *Adding it up: Helping children learn mathematics.* Washington, DC: National Academies Press.

Parrish, S. (2010). *Number talks: Helping children build mental math and computation strategies, grades K-5.* Math Solutions.

Peters, J. (2002). University-school collaboration: Identifying faulty assumptions. *Asia-Pacific Journal of Teacher Education, 30*(3), 14.

Taymans, J., Tindle, K., Freund, M., Ortiz, D., & Harris, L. (2012). Opening the black box: Influential elements of an effective urban professional development school. *Urban Education, 47*(1), 224–249.

Trachtman, R. (2007). Inquiry and accountability in professional development schools. *The Journal of Educational Research, 100*(4), 197–203.

Trent, J., & Lim, J. (2010). Teacher identity construction in school–university partnerships: Discourse and practice. *Teaching and Teacher Education, 26*(8), 1609–1618.

Zeichner, K. (2010). Rethinking the connections between campus courses and field experiences in college-and university-based teacher education. *Journal of Teacher Education, 61*(1–2), 89–99.

Zimpher, N. L., & Howey, K. R. (2005). The politics of partnerships for teacher education redesign and school renewal. *Journal of Teacher Education, 56*(3), 266–271.

BRIDGING THE THEME

Relationships Matter

Mikkaka Overstreet and Lori Norton-Meier

Anyone who has ever taken a course in education has heard extensively about the necessity of building relationships. Relationships are at the very heart of teaching and learning. Moreover, relationships are crucial to the success of most endeavors in society. No person, no business, no functioning collective of any kind can thrive without building relationships.

Clinical partnerships are founded on reciprocal relationships between universities, schools, and communities. The nature of these relationships determines the nature of the partnerships. Will there be surface-level engagement (worth great press, but not necessarily great impact), or will the parties involved manage the heavy work of building trust and a shared vision? In the previous chapter, Lateefah Id-Deen helped us to envision what relationships should and could look like in university-school partnerships. In the next chapter, Mikkaka Overstreet elucidates the process of building such relationships.

CHAPTER 5

Ball Pythons, Bartering and Building Community

Mikkaka Overstreet

Abstract

How do individuals navigate spaces and roles to make large-scale clinical partnerships work? At a large urban research university, faculty worked to build the processes and practices that were required to manage a working relationship with one of the country's largest school districts. After four consecutive semesters spending two days a week at one partnership school, one researcher finally began to feel like a part of the school community. How did she get there and why did it take so long? This chapter discusses the complicated nature of clinical partnerships and the "bartering" that was necessary to build a reciprocal relationship in which a university partner became a member of the school community.

Keywords

building community – clinical partnerships – teacher education – professional reciprocity

1   Overview

How do individuals navigate spaces and roles to make large-scale clinical partnerships work? At a large urban research university, faculty worked to build the processes and practices that were required to manage a working relationship with one of the country's largest school districts. After four consecutive semesters spending two days a week at one partnership school, one researcher finally began to feel like a part of the school community. How did she get there and why did it take so long? This chapter discusses the complicated nature of clinical partnerships and the "bartering" that was necessary to build a reciprocal relationship in which a university partner became a member of the school community.

2 Introduction

The gym full of children was absolutely silent in a way I hadn't yet heard. Most mornings, the rows of children were pretty attentive, but by the end of the morning's announcements they were understandably squirming and whispering. Today, though, they'd heard a few announcements, listened to an entire story, and were about to be dismissed. Yet they were completely engaged—leaning forward, breath collectively held, eyes alight with curiosity.

When I pulled the snake from his bag, the collective breath was let out in a gasp. There were a few squeals and giggles that were quickly stifled. The children had all heeded my warnings about making Severus comfortable by being quiet and respectful. They had learned quite a bit about him from the children's book I'd written about him, *Severus Comes Home*, and were eager to show their new knowledge as they got a chance to interact with him.

As they filed past on their way out of the gym, they had the option of touching him if they chose. I noted how they reached for his body, remembering what I had taught them about ball pythons' poor eyesight and how it would scare him if they reached for his head. I was amazed by how much new knowledge they had retained and were able to immediately apply when they were engaged this way.

One kindergartner summed up the experience much better than I could have. With a huge smile on his face he announced, "I never met a book character before! Now I met two—you and Severus!"

3 One Model of Clinical Partnerships

The College of Education (COE) at our university professes in its conceptual framework that "all candidates are expected to demonstrate knowledge, skills, and dispositions to affirm principles of social justice and equity and a commitment to making a positive difference." The COE's model of clinical partnership work is a direct response to this goal. The partnership aims "to eliminate disparities in education, health, economic development, and human/social services ... through an initiative in five schools" in the most economically disadvantaged area of the city. The COE provides resources, materials, and human capital to its partnership schools: COE faculty provide professional development and conduct research while COE students have practicum and student teaching experiences in these schools. The partnership schools allow the COE to have dedicated physical spaces in which to teach classes, collaborate with teachers, and support the schools in a variety of ways.

One use of the space involves holding methods classes within the partnership schools. Methods courses, often the bulk of most teacher education programs, provide students with both content knowledge and pedagogical skills. These courses are typically divided by subject area, with designations like "literacy methods" or "math methods." A unique benefit of holding such classes within a K-12 space is that preservice teachers (PSTs) are able to immediately observe and/or practice the teaching methods they are learning, and to discuss and reflect on those experiences under the guidance of their methods instructor (Dieker, Rodriguez, Lignugaris/Kraft, Hynes, & Hughes, 2014). As a clinical professor in the COE, I taught literacy methods within a partnership school. This chapter chronicles some of my experiences.

In addition to having physical space within our partnership schools, our model of clinical partnerships included two designated individuals to link the schools to the university. The teacher-in-residence (TiR) was a school employee who provided insider access to school structures. Working closely with the university liaison, a university employee assigned to each school, the TiR coordinated university-related activities, communicated on the university's behalf with teachers and staff, and had the option of co-teaching methods courses or co-facilitating school-based professional development (PD). These two roles (TiR and university liaison) were crucial to managing the complex structure of the partnerships, but their expectations and effectiveness varied by site.

Even with these people and structure in place, it took four consecutive semesters spending two days a week at one school before I, as a literacy methods instructor teaching my courses at Tubman Elementary School*, finally began to feel like a part of the school community. How did I get there and why did it take so long? In this chapter I'll discuss the complicated nature of clinical partnerships and the "bartering" that was necessary to build a reciprocal relationship in which I, as a university partner, became a member of the school community.

4   What We Know about Clinical Partnerships

Within the field of education there is a noted and long-lamented gap between research and practice, between K-12 schools and universities and, in teacher education, between educational theories and practical classroom application (Dieker et al., 2014; Durnan, 2016; Howell, Carpenter, & Jones, 2013; Korthagen, Loughran, & Russell, 2006). Clinical partnerships between schools and universities, in their varied forms, demonstrate one method for bridging these gaps (Howell, Carpenter, & Jones, 2013; Johnson, 2010). Clinical partnerships, in which K-12 partners are often referred to as professional development schools (PDS), ideally involve bringing university faculty and students into K-12 schools for the mutual benefit of both parties. This can take the form of university-led professional development for teachers, practicum and student teaching experiences for university students, research opportunities for university faculty, collaborations on innovative projects, university support for the school's larger community, and so on (Durnan, 2016; Howell, Carpenter, & Jones, 2013; Stillman & Anderson, 2017).

Unfortunately, such partnerships do not always go as planned. Often, the partnerships are one-sided, with universities reaping the most benefits. Placing too many practicum students or student teachers at one school, often without additional training in coaching adult learners, can be burdensome on teachers' time and abilities (Childre & Van Rie, 2015; Howell, Carpenter, & Jones, 2013). Further, while the university can positively frame these relationships as community engagement, the school staff does not always feel engaged. Too often university-led PD and other activities are planned with little input from teachers, leaving them feeling undervalued (Hodson & Jones, 2010).

When teachers feel they have a voice, partnerships between schools and universities are much more impactful (Hodson & Jones, 2010). In today's climate, teachers routinely feel frustrated by top-down policies enacted from the school, district, and even national level (ndunda, Van Sickle, Perry, & Capelloni, 2017). So-called partnerships with university staff who engage in the same oppressive practices only serve to alienate teachers and lay the groundwork for relationships that will, at best, result in surface-level compliance. Conversely, when university partners engage school staff as experts whose insights are invaluable to building a shared and student-centered vision, partnerships flourish and teachers come to the work with enthusiasm and investment (Knight, 2011; ndunda et al., 2017). True partnership requires a clear vision and structure, designed with all stakeholders at the table (Reischl, Khasnabis, & Karr, 2017).

When all parties are truly invested in the partnership, the outcomes are well worth the effort (Howell, Carpenter, & Jones, 2013). Stillman and Anderson (2017) describe one such partnership between a university and a high performing bilingual school:

> This multitiered school-university partnership generated benefit in both directions, with the university providing Playa with many of its excellent teachers and at least some of its professional development, and with Playa providing the university with a "model" bilingual school wherein its future teachers could see and "put into practice" the university's teachings. (p. 20)

This longstanding partnership between the school and university was actively cultivated by participants on both sides with a clear vision, who were willing to take the time it would require to bring their vision to fruition. Reischl, Khasnabis, and Karr (2017) assert that the work of partnering "deepens and changes over time" (p. 52) so it is important to enter such relationships with a clear, long-term commitment to the partnership. With the ultimate goal of improving teaching and learning, all parties must be invested in the effectiveness of the partnership, and that means committing to continuous improvement and evolution over time. In a complex climate of education reform, it is even more imperative that these partnerships are truly collaborative and involve all stakeholders in planning, implementation, facilitation, and evaluation in order to be successful and effectively utilize a shrinking pool of resources (Howell, Carpenter, & Jones, 2013).

5   Learning the Landscape

The summer before I began my work at Tubman Elementary School, two colleagues and I presented to the faculty during their summer PD. My colleagues had worked at Tubman before. I had not. As we talked about all we hoped to do—ideas for getting our preservice teachers involved with their students, projects we hoped to accomplish together, ways we hoped we could expand on the work they were doing and support their efforts—the Tubman teachers responded with varying degrees of disinterest. Several teachers talked amongst themselves. Most stared back silently. One or two asked questions or offered comments.

When one of my colleagues talked about work she'd done with a Tubman teacher that had been focused on connecting with the students' identities, I was fascinated. The young teacher was a graduate of our program and was taking risks by engaging the poor, predominantly Black students in her class in critical literacy, rather than sticking to the prescribed curriculum. My colleague talked about a project they'd collaborated on to learn the stories of the students' names. Passionately, my colleague proclaimed, "If you'd heard some of these stories and what their names meant to the families, you would never laugh at a student's name again."

A Tubman teacher whispered something to another. They both started laughing.

Later, when we talked about a writing strategy that involved written conversations around a text, we discovered that my students would be reading a novel that several of the fifth grade classes were reading as well. I offered several ideas for how we could collaborate so that all of our students could benefit from more deeply engaging with the text. I was greeted with noncommittal smiles (and, unsurprisingly, never managed to connect our classes on that project).

After the Tubman teachers left, my colleagues and I sat together and vented our frustrations. How were we supposed to work with these people?

The real question should have been how could we get these people to trust us? Tubman Elementary, one of our first partnership schools, had endured many of the negative aspects of partnerships described previously in this chapter. Nestled in the heart of one of the city's poorest neighborhoods, they had come into this partnership eager to take advantage of the resources such a relationship could offer. As the university figured out what exactly the partnership would entail, Tubman teachers and staff dealt with broken promises, top-down PD chosen and implemented by the university, and frequent personnel turnovers. In light of all they had seen over the years, why should they buy into anything we university people had to say?

Tubman teachers had learned to comply, without truly engaging. Why should they? Previous liaisons and other university staff had come in with big ideas, only to leave without actually seeing the ideas through. Worse, some had been condescending and determined to "fix" the teachers, offering insights and criticism without allowing the teachers much input or valuing their expertise. Despite ample research indicating that effective professional development experiences must promote teacher empowerment by allowing them voice and choice (Darling-Hammond, Wei, Andree, Richardson, & Orphanos, 2009; Overstreet, 2017; Stewart, 2014), some previous university staff had instead simply decided what the Tubman teachers needed and delivered PD accordingly. These teachers had been burned and they were not going to be easily won over again.

Further complicating the relationship between university representatives and school staff was the current climate in the school. Tubman's overall accountability score, based on student performance on standardized tests, was at 54.0 when I began my relationship with the school—well below the state's proficiency cut score of 67.2. The school also had "gap group" students (e.g. students of color, emergent bilingual students, students from poverty, or students with disabilities) scoring in the bottom 5% in the state. Consequently, the school was under intense scrutiny and immense pressure to increase test scores each year so as not to be at risk of takeover by the state department of education. School administrators had enacted several new programs and adopted new curricula in an attempt to meet these demands.

This pressure was apparent in Tubman's environment. At the start of each day, the entire school assembled in the gym for a morning meeting. This amazing opportunity to build community was often eclipsed by reports of achievement data and, since school leadership knew that attendance was tied to achievement, daily charting of student attendance. No amount of promised celebrations and cheerful insistence that they do their part could engage and excite five-year-olds about a bar graph of absences at 8:30 in the morning. The teachers appeared even less enthused.

Considering all of these factors, it was no wonder Tubman's teachers were not thrilled to welcome more outsiders with additional expectations and ideas. If we were going to make any progress, we would have to earn their trust. According to Reischl, Khasnabis, and Karr (2017), ongoing trust building is an essential aspect of this work. University partners, who usually have more flexible schedules, have to be creative in making the time to talk with teachers and finding meaningful ways to support them. Despite the challenges ahead of me, I began to think about how I could build the types of relationships necessary to a mutually beneficial partnership.

6   Compliance, But Not Community

> *Excitedly, I drafted an email. I remembered being a classroom teacher and imagined what I could've done with the offer of 25 extra pairs of adult hands. There were so many innovative projects we could attempt together. I asked the teachers for ideas on what they would like to do, what topics they were interested in exploring, what would be helpful to them, and what standards my students should address during the agreed upon "buddy time" with their elementary school partners.*
>
> *I did not receive a response. I waited. And waited. After a week or so, I followed up with the TiR who had been copied on my original email. She responded promptly, promising to follow up with the classroom teachers.*
>
> *Soon, I received another email from her with the teachers' responses. It was a list of standards they were working on and/or students were having trouble with. Beyond that, I was told they were open to whatever I wanted to do.*

My first two semesters of teaching at Tubman can only be described as "meh." Admittedly, the lackluster experience was at least 50% my fault—and that's a conservative estimate. Fresh out of my PhD program and with no experience teaching undergraduates or methods courses, I had a highly theoretical approach that was as impractical as it was developmentally inappropriate. The PSTs in my charge needed concrete pedagogical content knowledge and I was busily trying to engage them in deep discussions critiquing an educational system they didn't yet understand.

The first teacher we partnered with, Ms. F, had worked with the previous literacy methods instructor and allowed the students to do their major assignment for the course in her classroom. It was a highly structured case study that required PSTs to observe one student across various settings and assess the student's literacy strengths and needs. It required that Ms. F plan for our visits carefully to ensure that we would see specific types of instruction; this required that she change her schedule to work around our needs. I decided that this was too demanding, required my students to do their case study elsewhere, and told Ms. F that we would be happy to do whatever she wanted us to do.

In retrospect, this approach was no less demanding than the other. Now Ms. F had to plan (with me if our schedules allowed) for activities we could "help with." Since, as Reischl, Khasnabis and Karr (2017) assert, "demands on teachers' time have probably never been greater, and it can be challenging to find opportunities to talk together" (p. 52), it's no surprise that Ms. F did most of the planning. My students spent a disconnected series of sessions with their elementary buddies doing everything from simply reading together to conducting writing conferences. I knew that things had not gone well (even before I received my brutally honest teaching evaluations):

> *The semester is drawing to a close and I'm wondering what my students are taking away from the class. I feel like I didn't maximize the effectiveness of their time with students—they met with their buddies each week, but we didn't have an ongoing project or anything and often spent the 45 minutes on something different the teacher wanted to do each week, with the remainder of the time reading with the kids. I know it was important to support the work going on in the classroom, but I believe that it would've been more helpful to have a long-term goal and more structure for that time. I need to look at the larger goals of the class and think about what experiences I want to foster next semester.* (Teacher Reflection Journal, December 1, 2015)

Despite this reflection, I did not do much better the following semester. I partnered with several teachers instead of just Ms. F, but the other teachers were less experienced with the partnership model and were much less enthusiastic than Ms. F (notably a recent graduate of our program) had been. Sometimes they forgot we were coming and we spent part of our time waiting for them to hastily wrap up another activity. Again, nobody had a long-term project or big idea they wanted us to work on together. They let us borrow their children, but we were not a part of their classrooms.

The Tubman teachers had given us standards to work on so, after modeling some lesson planning strategies, I had my students plan their weekly partner reading time around those standards. They used a simple frame of before/during/after reading. I never checked their lesson plans and we debriefed only superficially. Though the children and even some of the teachers seemed happy to see us each week, I was not sure my PSTs were learning much.

Kirschenbaum and Reagan (2001) noted that "the greatest frustrations ... in regard to collaboration revolved around inconsistent commitment to the collaboration by school personnel, poor communication, and lack of shared program development and ownership" but wisely added that "school personnel no doubt sometimes share these feelings and perceptions regarding their university partners" (p. 501). What was I doing to demonstrate my commitment to an ongoing relationship and what could I be doing differently? It was time to change my own actions and take more responsibility for the partnership.

7   Give, Give, Give, and Take

This was something to smile about.

We were engaging the students and teachers at Tubman. They were happy. We weren't asking anything in return.

Our literacy team had planned an African American Read-In—a week of activities highlighting works authored by and/or about Black people. Every child was going to hear quality literature read aloud and every classroom was going to have a copy of a good "mirror" text, a book that the majority Black students at Tubman could see themselves reflected in.

It had been a lot of work on our side, but we'd finally done something to put a dent in the deficit we owed this school community.

It started with a casual conversation with the Tubman liaison. As fellow literacy instructors and friends, Tammi and I often reflected together on our experiences at Tubman. During a routine conversation, I randomly mentioned how an administrative assistant in another office had recently completed a task that was going to take me days to do on my own. All I had done was ask him a question about the task and, since he had more access to the data I needed as well as more time, he just decided to do it for me. I was so grateful and he was pleased that something he considered simple had helped me so much.

Tammi looked thoughtful after my story. "That's what we need to do at Tubman. We need to do more things that we can do easily, but they can't. We need to do things to lighten their load."

This simple observation became a turning point for me in relationship with Tubman's staff. I emailed everyone and reiterated my offers to take on big ideas and projects, but also mentioned that I was going to be spending a few hours after my classes twice a week to just be present at Tubman, instead of leaving right after I taught. If there was anything I could help with during that time, I told them I would be happy to do so.

It was a slow process. Often, I spent those hours grading and planning, which meant that I could rationalize spending more time at the school without thinking about the many other tasks on my to-do list. In between the teaching tasks, though, I started making my presence known. I left snacks in the break room. I wandered the halls, speaking to people and helping with any little chore I noticed—stapling fallen items back onto bulletin boards, checking on kids in bathrooms, helping teachers carry armfuls of books and materials. Eventually, someone responded to my email and requested help in the understaffed early childhood classrooms. I started popping into those classrooms each week and sending students to help as well.

My small efforts couldn't balance out the "giving deficit" we had racked up. These teachers and this school had given so much that it would take more than a little manual labor to build reciprocity. The literacy team and I started to think bigger.

One of our biggest undertakings was the African-American Read-in (AARI). Annually, the AARI took place at sites around the country. Its focus was on highlighting works by and about African-Americans, to counteract centuries of the marginalization of Black people in literature. We decided that we would plan an AARI at Tubman:

1. One week in February will be selected for AA Read-In Week.
2. [U]ndergrads will be partnered with classes during designated times on Mon-Thurs to read in small groups.
3. There will be a kickoff event which will take place on the Monday of that week within the morning meeting (media and other publication outlets will be notified about event). Each day of the week a different person will "guest star" for morning meeting to highlight AA literacy in multiple ways—Tytianna read aloud, MK Storytelling …
4. There will be a total of 6 different AA authored books chosen, one for each grade level k-5. Bianca will send out a book list recommendation to all invested parties prior to final approval.
5. Tammi will talk with [principal] about scheduling/timing and other logistical matters (African-American Read-In plan, February 6, 2016).

One of our biggest undertakings to date, the AARI was a massive success. Each morning, university staff (including literacy instructors, the COE dean, and the university president) conducted activities during the school-wide morning meeting. Over the course of the week, all classes were visited by PSTs, who read to the Tubman students from the children's books the university had purchased for the school and led the students in completing reading responses.

The AARI added to the relationship I was building with the school community. After leading two morning meetings and showcasing my talents as a storyteller and snake lover, the entire school knew who I was finally. My pet snake, Severus, and I were invited to visit individual classrooms and to participate in the schools' summer activities. My PSTs and I were more sought after as partners and the next semester we had a team of close-knit and enthusiastic first grade teachers to partner with.

Howell, Carpenter, and Jones (2013) warn that building true partnerships is "very time consuming and bears an emotional cost that most do not anticipate" (p. 48). My experience at Tubman illustrated the veracity of that statement. It was far less exhausting when I had simply shown up, taught my classes, and communicated with teachers via email as needed. However, I had never before felt so accepted at Tubman.

8 Reflections and Implications

I moved through the hall quickly and easily now. I no longer thought about the path to a particular room or had to search my mind for a teacher's name. This place had become familiar to me.

As I passed a line of students, many smiled and waved. One girl whispered shyly to her teacher, who laughed and waved me over.

"Tell her what you told me," smiled the teacher.

"You're the snake lady," the little girl told me confidently. "You read your book to us this summer and we met your snake."

"You recognized me even though I've changed my hair?" I asked, fingering the long braids I'd recently substituted for my normal short Afro. "I thought I was in disguise!"

The little girl giggled. "I will always recognize you!"

It seemed I had finally become a part of the school.

Leaving any job can be bittersweet, but one of my first thoughts after I accepted a new position, was about the teachers at Tubman. Just when we'd gotten to a place of mutual understanding, I was leaving like so many others before me. I thought about the dynamic young Mrs. H who had begun to talk to me in snatched moments about her worries as a new teacher, trusting me with her vulnerabilities. I remembered the super-organized Ms. R who now included me in her sarcastic wit and conspiratorial whispers. I thought about the brilliant teaching assistant who I was trying to convince to return to school for her teaching credentials. All those relationships I'd painstakingly built and now I was leaving.

No experience is wasted if we learn from it. It's even more meaningful if others can learn from our experiences as well. Thus, I leave you with a few parting thoughts:

1. *Put in the time.* This work is ultimately about relationships and those can't be built without trust borne of shared commitment.
2. *Build a shared vision.* Again, the best partnerships involve all stakeholders constructing shared goals and expectations. If the vision and expectations for reaching the vision are clear, partnerships will be able to survive the inevitable personnel turnover that will occur in any long-term commitment.
3. *Be partners.* Perhaps this is just too obvious, but unless all parties approach the partnership with humility and an openness to learn, there will be imbalances of power that result in feelings of resentment. Teachers, administrators, and university staff should all consider each other as respected experts who bring unique insights to the work.

None of this was easy for me and if it comes easily to you, it's because somebody put in the work before you. As Howell, Carpenter, and Jones (2013) promised, it was worth the effort and I will likely continue to benefit from the experience for the rest of my career. I hope and believe my methods students and Tubman's teachers can say the same.

References

Childre, A., & Van Rie, G. (2015). Mentor teacher training: A hybrid model to promote partnering in candidate development. *Rural Special Education Quarterly, 34*(1), 10–16.

Darling-Hammond, L., Wei, R. C., Andree, A., Richardson, N., & Orphanos, S. (2009). *Professional learning in the learning profession.* Washington, DC: National Staff Development Council.

Dieker, L., Rodriguez, J., Lignugaris/Kraft, B., Hynes, M., & Hughes, C. (2014). The potential of simulated environments in teacher education: Current and future possibilities. *Teacher Education and Special Education, 37*(1), 21–33.

Durnan, V. (2016). Cases in partnership between independent schools and universities. *Peabody Journal of Education, 91*(5), 691–710.

Hodson, P., & Jones, D. (2010). The construction of primary teachers' subject knowledge in English: An enquiry into teaching partnerships between universities and schools. *International Journal of Learning, 17*(7), 59–70.

Howell, P. B., Carpenter, J., & Jones, J. P. (2013). School partnerships and clinical preparation at the middle level. *Middle School Journal, 44*(4), 40–49.

Johnson, D. (2010). Learning to teach: The influence of a university-school partnership project on pre-service elementary teachers' efficacy for literacy instruction. *Reading Horizons, 50*(1), 23–48.

Kirschenbaum, H., & Reagan, C. (2001). University and urban school partnerships: An analysis of 57 collaborations between a university and a city school district. *Urban Education, 36*(4), 479–504.

Knight, J. (2011). What good coaches do. *Educational Leadership, 69*(2), 18–22.

Korthagen, F., Loughran, J., & Russell, T. (2006). Developing fundamental principles for teacher education programs and practices. *Teaching and Teacher Education, 22*(8), 1020–1041.

ndunda, m., Van Sickle, M., Perry, L., & Capelloni, A. (2017). University–urban high school partnership: Math and science professional learning communities. *School Science and Mathematics, 117*(3–4), 137–145.

Overstreet, M. (2017). Culture at the core: Moving from professional development to professional learning. *Journal of Ethnographic & Qualitative Research, 11*(3), 199–214.

Reischl, C. H., Khasnabis, D., & Karr, K. (2017). Cultivating a school-university partnership for teacher learning: A partnership between a research university and two schools in its community shows the power of collaboration to address achievement gaps while also preparing future teachers. *Phi Delta Kappan, 98*(8), 48.

Stewart, C. (2014). Transforming professional development to professional learning. *MPAEA Journal of Adult Education, 43*(1), 28–33.

Stillman, J., & Anderson, L. (2017). *Teaching for equity in complex times: Negotiating standards in a high-performing bilingual school.* New York, NY: Teachers College Press.

BRIDGING THE THEME

Stories Matter

Mikkaka Overstreet and Lori Norton-Meier

Stories are legitimate forms of reasoned knowledge.
WORTH (2008)

∴

In the introduction, we asserted the importance of stories. Already our authors have illustrated the ability of stories to both clarify and complicate our understandings. Stories are unique to their contexts, but collectively have the power to show us trends and truths we might not see otherwise. Worth (2008) argues that in the reading, telling, and hearing of well-constructed narratives we experience and practice *narrative reasoning* and that leads to a more complex and comprehensive understanding of the human experience. When building a collective of stories that we can learn from, the characters are important. Who is telling the stories (and to what audience)? Whose voices are amplified? Whose voices are silenced? How might the missing voices change or trouble our current understandings?

In the previous chapter, Mikkaka Overstreet shared stories from her efforts to forge relationships in a clinical partnership setting. In the next chapter, Tammi Davis features voices we've not yet heard in this collection of stories—that of the preservice teachers. Davis shares the stories of four PSTs to provide another perspective on the impact of school-university partnerships.

Reference

Worth, S. E. (2008). Storytelling and narrative knowing: An examination of the epistemic benefits of well-told stories. *Journal of Aesthetic Education, 43*(3), 42–56.

CHAPTER 6

From Saviors to Safety Nets: How a Unique Semester Helped Preservice Teachers Think More Deeply about Their Field Placements and Coursework

Tammi R. Davis

Abstract

This collective case study examines the journey of four teacher candidates' experiences in a university partnership school where a university faculty member was their methods instructor, field supervisor, and partnered with the teacher in residence and other block instructor in an effort to provide students with a connected and deep experience in the school and community. The primary sources were an end of the semester reflective assignment and a focus group interview with the four participants. Using metaphoric analysis, I unveil the implicit metaphors of each of the four students in this journey. Findings include how the collective stories of these four teacher candidates can inform teacher educators to find ways to assist their teacher candidates by (1) making explicit the connections between course, fieldwork, and assignments, (2) valuing the importance of assisting teacher candidates in feeling a part of the school and neighborhood community, and (3) understanding the importance of guiding students from sympathy to empathy of students and communities.

Keywords

urban field placement – professional development school – teacher education – faculty in professional development schools

1   Overview

This collective case study examines the journey of four preservice teachers' (PSTs) experiences in an urban university partnership school where a university faculty member was their methods instructor, field supervisor, and partnered with the teacher in residence and other university faculty member in an effort to enhance TC's immersion in the local school's context to allow them to know students more deeply and to build stronger professional mentoring relationships with teachers in the building, in the school, and the community. The primary sources were an end of the semester reflective assignment and a focus group interview with the four participants. Using thematic analysis, I unveil the themes associated with the experiences of the four participants. Findings include how the collective stories of these four PSTs highlighted (1) teachers as co-pilots; (2) students as sufficient; and (3) connection of the program dots. Based on these findings, discussion includes urging teacher education programs to prioritize collaboration with each other and schools and finally, to recognize the importance of elementary school students benefitting from university school partnerships.

2   Introduction

> I was excited and considered myself fortunate to be able to teach my undergraduate literacy methods course in a local elementary school. Each week I was able to facilitate conversations about literacy content and then walk down the hallways with my university students to elementary classrooms to work on projects with elementary students. The university students responded with equal enthusiasm as the semester progressed.
>
> However, it was in the before class chatter that I began to hear conversations like this: "Which reflection is that? We can't say anything similar about the week field placement reflection for class one and class two or we get a 0. Where do we do this assignment, in our field placement or in class?" As I listened to these types of questions and realized the stress and disconnections between various parts of the semester for students. I began to wonder what would happen if the students were able to experience more connections than disconnections in their first semester of their teacher education program. (Author's field notes, 2014)

Inspired by the opening scenario and many other conversations like it, I examined the courses and assignments our preservice teachers (PSTs) had in their first semester. Based on this examination, I reached out to a colleague who taught a course about community building and agreed to join me so we could teach both courses at the elementary school and also have PSTs assigned to that same school for their field placement. There, I and the Teacher in Residence (TiR) would serve as their field supervisors. In this model, the faculty members and TiR worked closely together to make sure assignments connected across classes and clear links were made between the classes and field experience. This chapter focuses on the pilot semester of this project as seen through the eyes of four focal preservice teachers (PSTs). Much has been written over the years about university lab schools, professional development schools, and clinical partnerships. These terms, along with others like them, are often defined differently and interchanged in multiple ways. For this chapter, I want to situate my review of literature by avoiding these labels, and instead reviewing, most easily tied to my work, learning about teaching in schools, and learning about teaching in urban contexts. Next, I will describe this study as experienced by the four focal PSTs using interviews and other class data. The identified themes are followed by a discussion of how these themes illuminate the possibilities for PSTs when more is done by faculty members to make clear links to their experiences. The overarching question that guided this study was: *How do PSTs experience a pilot program designed with multiple classes, their field experience, and three university faculty members as instructors and supervisors?*

3. Literature Review

3.1 *Learning about Teaching in Schools*

Multiple studies throughout the years have confirmed that school based courses and field experiences in schools produce beginning teachers that are more knowledgeable of schools and how they operate, more confident about themselves as teachers, and are more likely to be reflective practitioners (Abdal-Haqq, 1998; Rock & Levin, 2002; Thompson & Ross, 2000). Although school based field experiences have been enacted for decades, more recently arguments for innovations in preparation programs have been aimed at deeper immersion in practice. Many, Fisher, Ogletree, and Taylor's (2012) work spoke to my own desire to begin these types of immersions as early as the first semester of teacher preparation coursework. Dutro, Cartun, Melnychenko, Haberl, and Williams (2018), emphasize the power of "crisscrossing the university and public-school contexts as professional development school boundary spanners" and also drew attention to the calls for creative solutions to "wriggle free" from some of the structural barriers that had seemed so difficult to dismantle and just as importantly, saw their partnership as a path toward deeply intertwining practices of literacy teaching and critical lenses on justice (p. 2). Additionally, Dutro et al. (2018) found their partnership fostered "new ways of being for all involved," particularly pointing out "PSTs have opportunities to experience the complexities of teaching, enact a learning cycle of instruction, and develop deep relationships with children from the start of their preparation, with in-the-moment support from teacher educators" (p. 15).

This research project grew from our university commitment and professional understanding that situating university-based courses and field experiences in schools provides PSTs with opportunities to learn in schools. As Darling Hammond (2006) reminds us, the weaknesses of traditional program models are when they are collections of largely unrelated courses, adding credence to a low public regard for teacher education programs. Conversely, she argues that we have learned how to create stronger and more effective teacher education programs that entail a "tight coherence and integration among courses and between coursework and clinical work in schools, extensive and intensely supervised clinical work integrated with course work using pedagogies that link theory and practice." Equally important, she emphasized the value of creating "closer, proactive relationships with schools that serve diverse learners effectively and develop and model good teaching" (p. 300).

3.2 *Learning about Teaching Urban Contexts*

Fewer university-school partnerships have considered urban teacher preparation. Groulx's (2001) study found that students placed in urban elementary school contexts "changed their minds about the challenges of working with minority children" (p. 86). Wong and Glass's (2005) work found that students who had an urban placement were initially more committed to teaching in low-income and culturally diverse settings. In spite of this, Boyle-Baise and McIntyre (2008) suggest, even more so than the past, "attention to equity, diversity, family, and community needs to become an integral part of PDS principles, perspectives, and practice" (p. 326).

The Urban Immersion program by Stairs (2008), conceptualized around leading urban education scholars like Ladson-Billings (1995) and Donnell (2007), believe there is a specialized knowledge that new teachers to the urban context must develop to successfully teach in urban schools. Stairs' work determined the importance of the development of PSTs' knowledge of content and pedagogy, but more importantly, the need to develop their knowledge of the urban context and how to balance the multiple demands so that all students might learn and improve their life chances. I can relate to this first hand. For my first teaching job, I moved from a small town in the Midwest to a metropolitan area in the South where I taught in an urban area with no training or understanding about this complex context. Not surprisingly I found myself, like many of my peers, "putting my time in" to get to a better teaching location.

FROM SAVIORS TO SAFETY NETS 65

This background compels me to advocate for PSTs to be supported by faculty and not just placed in urban contexts, hoping that the mere experience will teach them.

4   Methods

4.1   *Participants, Setting, and Background*

Arvin Elementary is situated in a neighborhood with a longstanding reputation of violence, high unemployment, and low levels of academic achievement. It is also in a zip code that is part of our university and college's mission to serve. In the fall of 2015, when I conducted this study, there were approximately 350 students attending the school and 98% of children received free or reduced-price lunch.

This semester was a pilot for a programmatic shift from courses and field placements situated in different contexts (see Figure 6.1) to a model where we sought to make these courses and experiences as interrelated as possible and faculty were intentionally collaborative about assignments and the overall experience (see Figure 6.2). As faculty member one, I was the university liaison between the university and school (working closely with the principal), the Literacy Methods course instructor, and collaborated with faculty member two, who taught the community course. I also worked closely with the Teacher in Residence. At our university, the TiR was a full-time employee of the district who served as a liaison between the school and university. In this context, she attended and contributed to the methods course, coordinated community field trips, and assisted in supervising students in their field placement.

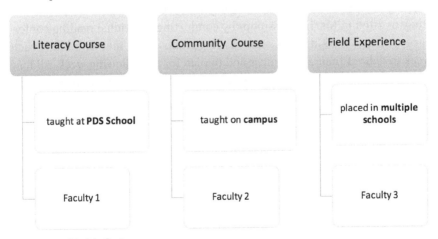

FIGURE 6.1   Model of prior program

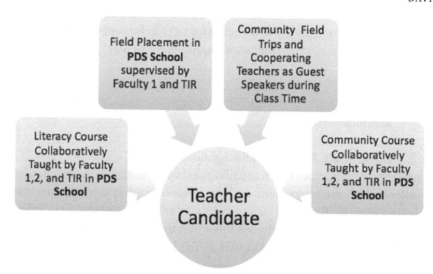

FIGURE 6.2   Model of pilot program

We taught 22 PSTs in their first semester of their professional program. Ninety percent identified as White and ten percent as Black. I also served as the university liaison to the school as well as the students' university supervisor. This was a pilot semester in which all 22 of my PSTs were also assigned to spend one half day per week in a classroom at Arvin Elementary (as opposed to traveling to multiple schools in the larger metropolitan area) in order to become immersed in the local school's context, to know students more deeply, and to build stronger professional mentoring relationships with teachers in the building. A typical day in the partnership setting is featured in Table 6.1.

These PSTs were juniors, yet in the first semester of the professional teaching program. On two field experience days, the four focal PSTs selected for this study assisted in Ms. H's classroom by conducting individual reading conferences and also working with small reading groups. They met with Ms. H each week to debrief their experiences and to plan for the following week. All four PSTs were of typical undergraduate age. Carol Jean, Betty, and Ruby identified as White and Jewel identified as Black.

4.2   *Data Collection and Analysis*

For this study, I collected the focal PSTs' written conference reflections, their final papers synthesizing what they learned over the course of the semester working with second graders, and arranged for another faculty member to conduct a focus group interview following the semester-long experience. The following question guided my analysis of data:

FROM SAVIORS TO SAFETY NETS

TABLE 6.1   Snapshot of a typical coursework day in our partnership

Time	Typical happenings
8:30–9:15	The TCs arrive at the school at 8:30 and begin their literacy coursework by discussing readings and relating them to sessions with second grade students for the day.
9:15–10:00	Prepare to meet with 2nd graders for writing conferences and gather materials.
10:00–11:00	TCs join 2nd graders for Writing Workshop. Second grade teacher or faculty member teaches mini-lesson and then TCs pair with 2nd graders for writing conferences and writing time.
11:00–11:30	TCs return to university classroom for debrief with faculty member and reflective writing time
11:30–12:00	Lunch
12:00–2:30	Afternoon Building and Learning Communities Course

How do PSTs experience a pilot program designed with multiple classes, their field experience, and three university faculty members as instructors and supervisors?

I conducted three rounds of data analysis. The first round was an initial or "pre-coding" (Layder, 1998, cited by Saldana, 2009), which mainly involved highlighting significant words and phrases. In the second round, I organized the data by participant (i.e. final reflective assignment and interview data) and conducted a line-by-line coding of these data in which I used descriptive and in vivo coding. This closer look at data allowed me to derive a deeper meaning from each (Saldaña, 2009). The descriptive coding allowed me to identify basic topics in the data that sometimes evolved into themes. The in vivo codes were used to identify words or phrases used by participants to capture significant ideas. For example, one participant used the word "intertwined" to describe her experience which became a theme that repeated in other areas of data.

For the third round of analysis, I conducted a cross-case analysis for recurring themes. Finally, using the developing themes from this round of analysis as the lens, I returned to the data to identify the most salient themes, refine themes if needed, and to assist me in the reporting of my findings. Three major themes were identified from my analysis: (1) teachers as co-pilots; (2) students as sufficient; and (3) connecting the program dots.

5   Findings

In this section I will report the three major themes revealed which were: (1) teachers as co-pilots; (2) students as sufficient; and (3) connecting the program dots. For each of these themes I will provide illustrative quotes from the participants. For an overview of the findings and a visual of how they are interconnected, see Figure 6.3.

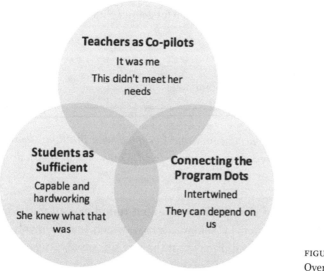

FIGURE 6.3
Overview of findings

5.1   *Teachers as Co-Pilots*

Throughout, the PSTs' reflections, observation notes, and group interview, the PSTs noted a shift in how they viewed their role as a teacher. The PSTs were beginning to view their role in the process, instead of only viewing the students' lack of knowledge. They recognized the importance of letting students be a partner in constructing their own knowledge.

"*It was me.*" In her project reflection Betty stated, "it took a few times of blank stares to realize *it was me* that was not giving clear directions instead of the student not understanding my directions." Similarly, Carol Jean, reflecting on her work with a student, said, "she [the second grader] took total control, ... I had to stop myself from intervening to give her the chance to 'do her thing.'" Carol Jean recognized the importance of letting the student take charge of her

FROM SAVIORS TO SAFETY NETS 69

own learning, and step back herself when she made the comment, "I learned from this project it is the student's work, not mine, so I need to let them be the pilot and take on the role of copilot that is there to assist them when they need it."

"This didn't meet her needs." Jewel had a shift in her thinking as she reviewed her own teaching practices with her 2nd grader. She recognized her initial techniques were not working when she stated,

> I would ask guiding questions sooner if I could do it again, instead of trying to give her some sort of motivational speech. I really wanted to motivate her in a way that was really rational and encouraging to me, however, this didn't meet her needs. She wasn't simply discouraged or unmotivated, she was overwhelmed.

Ruby had a similar experience with the student she was working with. In the story recounted below she recognized that creating a dialogue with the student was a more effective teaching technique than sharing an analogy that the student did not relate to.

> I explained to my student that we had a sandwich to make. The bread is our beginning and end, the meat is our middle, and the lettuce, tomato, mayonnaise was the "extras" that made our sandwich taste even better. She wasn't really following me, but I tried. To get her to think about more than 'my mom braided my hair', I asked her if her mom decorated her hair with beads, I asked her what color those beads were, I asked her if she went outside with her hair like that, how the wind felt when it blew in it, etc. I believe asking her those questions helped her decide how her story was going to layout.

These data excerpts highlighted the finding that this deeply immersed program helped PSTs recognize the importance of assisting and facilitating learning instead of merely imparting knowledge. Working alongside children this early in the program helped them begin to understand the importance of this type of thinking.

5.2 *Students as Sufficient*

Additionally, the PSTs' data highlighted a shift in how they viewed students. When PSTs recalled their feelings at the beginning of the semester a sampling of their comments was, "I honestly was rather nervous about being at this school [in the] location it is in and the reputation of the neighborhood" and "students were way smarter than I originally went in there thinking." The comments below showcase how student's thinking began to shift from students they were fearful to work with to more affirming views.

"Capable and Hardworking." Carol Jean describes the students in the classroom we partnered with like this, "I think it's like they're more than capable. They're great kids. They're intelligent students. Likewise, Betty talked about her experience with 2nd graders in this way:

> I also learned that both of the students were way smarter than I originally went in there thinking. Being able to observe the student beforehand gave me a preconceived idea about how the conferences would go. I was completely wrong in my pre-judgment. The students were brilliant in my eyes and were much more hardworking than I had ever imagined they would be during my time spent with each of them.

"She knew what that was." It was interesting, especially in a portion of an assignment that asked PSTs what surprised them about their experiences working with 2nd grade students, to find multiple comments where students were surprised about the prior knowledge students possessed. For example, Betty stated, "I was surprised that the student had so much detail in her story. This was in the very first meeting and she wrote about her weekend at the farm. She told me (and wrote about) the flavor of her ice cream without any conferencing." Additionally, Betty said, "she included several pieces of dialogue from her mother ... I loved that she knew what that was and I told her how awesome I thought it was that she included that."

Similarly, when the PSTs began working one-on-one with second graders their attitude shifted from being nervous to admiring the students' focus and work ethic. For example, Jewel stated, "I was surprised at how focused she was and how proud she was about her work. We stopped discussing so we could get words on our paper. The student took total control which I had to stop myself from intervening to give her the chance to "do her thing."

These data excerpts showcased the finding that this deeply immersed program helped PSTs view students in affirming ways related to their academic abilities and work ethic. Listening carefully to children helped PSTs value how much children already bring to their writing and they began to step aside a bit to let the students shine on their own.

5.3 Connecting the Program Dots

In a pilot semester where PSTs were intentionally deeply immersed in a school and community, it would be expected for them to gain deeper insights about their role as teachers and the students they worked with. However, PSTs also talked about how this experience seemed connected for them and how it not only benefitted them, but how they recognized the benefits for elementary students.

"Intertwined." It was Ruby's comments in the end of the semester interview that helped me gain insights about how the pilot semester was experienced by PSTs. She said, "I feel like they [classes and field experiences] really have gotten to be intertwined. Dr. Davis knows our classroom and when in one of my [reading] responses I was talking about trying to figure out how to not engage in a power struggle [with second graders] and what other tools I could use ... she [was] able comment back 'I'm really interested to see how you do that.' " Later, Ruby said, "she [Dr. Davis] is able to specifically help me [with classroom situations]. We can actually get a much better idea of what it's going to be like to be a teacher when we can exercise those things that we're learning in class in the classroom because we're consistently with them and we know these students."

Ruby appreciated her relationship with her cooperating teacher and expressed this by saying, "She [Mrs. H] is consistently giving us more and more responsibility because she knows us. So, I think that we have gotten to exercise our teacher muscles a lot more and really grow in ways that we couldn't if we weren't in the building with them and if Dr. Davis didn't know our kids and was able to help us in that way .... I think that this will be foundational for all of us." And finally, she said, "it's been amazing. It's been better than any field placement I've ever had. I feel like they really have gotten to be *intertwined.*"

"They can depend on us." It was particularly interesting to find multiple data points where PSTs expressed how they thought the pilot semester benefited the elementary students. Carol Jean recounted a key moment for her by saying, "during a lesson about listening and responding to each other's hair stories, one of the students in my group said 'it doesn't matter if you always look beautiful, as long as you're here.'" This had a great impact on Carol Jean which was evident when she stated, "When those words came out of that little boy's mouth, I teared up. I realized that when you harness a student's abilities, instead of holding them back because they sometimes misbehave, you help them make the most out of their career as a student and can really change their life."

Likewise, Betty stated, "it's really good for the students. We're not coming and going, really. We're there. We're there Mondays and Thursdays, ... we're there for them. They know that we're going to be there. *They can depend on us.* "Also, Jewel said, "The kids know us, the staff knows us, the teachers know us ... they know we have expectations for them and their setting expectations for us." These data points highlighted the finding that this immersed program benefitted children in how the PSTs not only saw students relying on them, but also that elementary students began to set expectations for the PSTs that became a part of their classroom community.

Finally, Jewel said, "So it's really nice to just come to a school, our class is right there and students that we love and we've been around throughout this entire semester are right around the corner. And *we're always there for them.*"

5.4 *Limitations and Implications*

As a researcher, I recognize that examination of data from four students in one semester provides only a small glimpse of what is possible when faculty members are intentional about working closely together with elementary staff and each other to make sure assignments are connected across classes and clear links are made between the classes and field experience. Absent from this study are the voices of the other faculty members, the school personnel, and administration who played a large part in making this experience beneficial for students. This focused glimpse, through the eyes of my undergraduate students, however, has prompted me to recognize when students have experiences in schools where they feel a part of the community they have the potential to grow as teachers and learners. I also recognize these findings are not generalizable to other populations beyond these four PSTs.

Despite these limitations, this study underscores Darling Hammond's (2006) assertion for teacher educators to strive for closer, proactive relationships with schools serving diverse learnes. In an era where university budgets are being cut, it is important to point out that this experience would not have been possible without the long-term commitment that the university and school had to each other. Additionally, colleges that encourage faculty members to work in and with schools also make experiences like these possible. This sometimes becomes a challenge when tenure track faculty may be seen as more successful for numbers of publications over working closely in schools.

Reflecting on the analysis and findings from the experiences of Carol Jean, Betty, Ruby, and Jewel, I leave this study inspired to provide in school experiences where PSTs are provided opportunities early in their professional programs to deepen their perceptions of themselves as teachers and envision students in any school setting as capable and eager to learn. Additionally, this project has spurred me to think about ways that teacher education programs can prioritize collaboration with each other and schools. Finally, this pilot project taught me to acknowledge the often-overlooked seriousness of the elementary school student benefitting from university school partnerships.

5.5 *Co-Piloting Capable Learners*

The four PSTs' stories in this study reminded me of the importance of being in schools. As Darling Hammond (2006) says, "It is impossible to teach people how to teach powerfully by asking them to imagine what they have never seen" (p. 308). Although I can't be certain, I believe that a semester in a university classroom would not have caused these students to come away from a semester understanding that the students, that some might perceive as "struggling" and "below grade level writers," are capable and eager learners, while simultaneously recognizing the power of them coming alongside these students to co-pilot them through learning experiences. Bien and Selland (2018) posit that "The goal of teacher education is to move teaching practice forward. This process, however, can be slow. It is nuanced. And the crunch of time and the urgency of contextual demands often make it seem necessary to shift focus from preparing teachers for a lifetime of practice to preparing teachers, instead, for tomorrow" (p. 93). I have attended faculty meetings where we discuss difficult decisions about classes and budgets. Having classes in schools is not the easiest or most cost-effective method. It was imperative for this pilot semester to keep this class size below 24 as to not oversaturate the school and to provide the optimal experience for the PSTs. My experiences with this pilot program support Bien and Selland's notion that time and contextual demands (and budgets and lack of faculty) often tempt us to lose sight of the fact we should be "preparing teachers for a lifetime of practice" instead of preparing "teachers for tomorrow" (p. 93). This includes taking the time and making sacrifices to ensure that students have as many opportunities as possible to learn about teaching in schools with faculty support.

5.6 *"We Are There for Them"*
Whether you have been a part of a university school partnership or not, I am sure you can imagine that these relationships do not come without their messy moments and challenges. Too often the focus shifts from elementary school learners to items like competition between schools, relationships between the adults in the elementary school building, and sometimes a partnership fatigue in which parties on both sides are "doing the work" but might lose sight of the why and especially the benefits for the school in particular. Since partnerships are commonly initiated and evaluated by universities rather than schools, research on the effectiveness of these efforts is often focused on the benefits to the university students rather than to the host schools (e.g., Darling-Hammond & Baratz-Snowden, 2007).

Sadly, I would add, besides the emphasis on "more hands in the building" to help raise test scores, we can potentially lose sight of the elementary aged learners due to this complex partnership. As Dutro et al. (2018) reminds us in partnerships, "Children are positioned as knowledgeable learners and as experts who are helping teachers learn" (p. 15).

I found it a very mature insight for students in the first semester of their teacher education program to recognize how students could trust them, depend on them, and know that they were "there for them." Most often PSTs begin their program with the focus on themselves and gradually work toward thinking of the learner in the teacher-student relationship. However, in this situation, likely because the semester was designed for them to build stronger professional mentoring relationships with teachers in the building, in the school, and the community the focal students were able to navigate the complexities around teaching, learning and putting the child in the center of their thinking. One of the key affordances of the pilot program was the depth of relationships it fostered. Spending a full day together with preservice teachers each week along with visiting them another day while they were in classrooms as they worked with children allowed me to support the connections between candidates and children in ways that would be impossible if their class and field experiences were located in separate spaces.

6   Final Thoughts

Research examining the impact of differing field-based experiences has been characterized as sparse at best (Shanahan, 2008) and I would also contend that sometimes the many hours per semester PSTs spend in elementary classrooms with little or sometimes even no university or faculty supervision often greatly decreases the potential rich learning experience for PSTs. Additionally, the presumption or myth persists that all field experiences result in positive consequences for PSTs (Zeichner, 1980). This is especially true when PSTs "fulfill" a "diversity placement" where on their own, they navigate the very placement in which they need the most scaffolding and support. I have seen this result in reinforcing deficit views of children and sometimes even "scaring" them out of the profession. While the field experience research base is not extensive, teacher preparation programs must recognize that more systematically structured, intensive field experiences prioritizing faculty involvement and research are necessary.

As Christopher Emdin (2016) emphasizes, many teacher education candidates internalize a vision of a the "savior complex where kids need to be saved" which equates to thinking something's wrong with these students. If educators are walking into classrooms and see students as victims, they are seeing them as having an inherent flaw that only educators can fix. Emdin emphasizes that the educator should be there "to help them learn and allow them to do fixing for themselves" (Emdin, 2016, para. 8). I believe the PSTs from the study semester were beginning to leave a S*avior* complex ideology and were viewing themselves as more of *Safety Net*. They were beginning to trust that elementary students in this urban environment were monitoring their own learning and saw themselves as sitting alongside them and being there to support, assist, and *catch them if they fall.*

Since implementing this pilot program, I have moved to another university. I find myself, for the first time in my 10 years as a teacher educator teaching my courses on campus either without a required field component or a field component I have very little connection with. I admit there are aspects of teaching this way that are simpler for me and my students. My student feedback on evaluations has been about great books that I introduced them to or even how much they enjoyed my teaching and passion for education, instead of about how they learned about children from children. The experiences and words of Carol Jean, Betty, Jewel, and Ruby linger with me and serve as an impetus for me to seek ways to get back into the more complex and messy work of partnering with teachers and schools, so that I can end semesters with evaluation comments like this from Jewel who said, "We're there for them."

References

Abdal-Haqq, I. (1998). *Professional development schools: Weighing the evidence*. Thousand Oaks, CA: Corwin Press.

Bien, A., & Selland, M. (2018). Living the stories, we tell: The sociopolitical context of enacting teaching stories. *Teaching and Teacher Education, 69*, 85–94.

Boyle-Baise, M., & McIntyre, D. J. (2008). What kind of experience? Preparing teachers in PDS or community settings. In M. Cochran-Smith, S. Feiman-Nemser, D. J. McIntyre, & K. E. Demers (Eds.), *Handbook of research on teacher education: Enduring questions in changing contexts* (3rd ed., pp. 307–329). New York, NY: Routledge and the Association of Teacher Educators.

Darling-Hammond, L. (2006). Constructing 21st-century teacher education. *Journal of Teacher Education, 57*(3), 300–314.

Darling-Hammond, L. (2014). Strengthening clinical preparation: The holy grail of teacher education. *Peabody Journal of Education, 89*(4), 547–561.

Darling Hammond, L., & Baratz Snowden, J. (2007). A good teacher in every classroom: Preparing the highly qualified teachers our children deserve. *Educational Horizons, 85*(2), 122–132.

Donnell, K. (2007). Getting to we: Developing a transformative urban teaching practice. *Urban Education, 42*(3), 223–249.

Dutro, E., Cartun, A., Melnychenko, K., Haberl, E., & Williams, B. P. (2018). Designing for critical, relational, practice-immersed teacher preparation: Weaving threads into tapestry in a critical project-based literacy partnership. *The New Educator, 14*(3), 1–18.

Emdin, C. (2016, July 18). *Author's advice to white teachers in urban schools: Drop the 'savior complex' and learn from students* [Interview by M. Elie]. Retrieved May 29, 2018, from http://neatoday.org/2016/07/18/chris-emdin/

Groulx, J. G. (2001). Changing preservice teacher perceptions of minority schools. *Urban Education, 36*(1), 60–92.

Ladson-Billings, G. (1995). Toward a theory of culturally relevant pedagogy. *American Educational Research Journal, 32*(3), 465–491.

Many, J. E., Fisher, T. R., Ogletree, S., & Taylor, D. (2012). Crisscrossing the university and public-school contexts as professional development school boundary spanners. *Issues in Teacher Education, 21*(2), 83–102.

Rock, T. C., & Levin, B. B. (2002). Collaborative action research projects: Enhancing pre-service teacher development. *Teacher Education Quarterly, 29*(1). 7–12.

Saldaña, J. (2009). *The coding manual for qualitative researchers*. Los Angeles, CA: Sage.

Shanahan, C. H. (2008). Essential fieldwork for the preparation of teachers of reading for urban settings. In L. C. Wilkinson, L. M. Morrow, & V. Chou (Eds.), *Improving literacy achievement in urban schools: Critical elements in teacher preparation*. Newark, DE: International Reading Association.

Stairs, A. (2010). Becoming a professional educator in an urban school-university partnership: A case study analysis of preservice teacher learning. *Teacher Education Quarterly, 37*(3), 45–62.

Thompson, S., & Ross, F. (2000). Becoming a teacher in a professional development school. *Teaching and Change, 8*(1), 31–50.

Wong, P., & Glass, R. (2005). Assessing a professional development school approach to preparing teachers for urban schools serving low-income, culturally and linguistically diverse communities. *Teacher Education Quarterly, 32*(3), 63–77.

Zeichner, K. M. (1980) Myths and realities: Field-based experiences in preservice teacher education. *Journal of Teacher Education, 31*(6), 45–49, 51–55.

BRIDGING THE THEME

Identity Matters

Mikkaka Overstreet and Lori Norton-Meier

In the previous chapter, Tammi Davis shared what she learned while helping her preservice teachers (PSTs) grapple with the ways they viewed themselves and the second grade students with whom they were working. She found that when they moved from viewing themselves as "saviors" educating disadvantaged youths to seeing themselves as "safety nets" in place to support students as needed, the shift in their perceptions of their own identities helped them to reject deficit perspectives of the children in the partnership school.

Much research has problematized the ways in which PSTs frame their experiences in high-poverty schools. Some of most widely respected education researchers have asserted that teacher candidates often enter their programs with lowered expectations for students of color, English language learners, and students who are academically disadvantaged (Darling-Hammond, 2010; Ladson-Billings, 2000; Nieto, 2010). These deficit perspectives impact the PSTs' instructional decisions, disciplinary actions, and shape their interactions with students.

Bianca Nightengale-Lee builds on this literature, and Tammi Davis' chapter, by sharing her work on deconstructing identity with PSTs. Using intersectionality as a lens, Nightengale-Lee complicates PSTs' understanding of themselves and others. In this space, we allow her to speak candidly, to share her "truths in relation to other Women of Color in academia, to document the intersections of [her] experiences with established literature, and to offer insights to shape future discourse" (Overstreet, 2019, p. 19). As Grey and Williams-Farrier (2017) said, "it is through the naming and voicing of these narratives that we remind the academy of the humanity of Black women" (p. 507). Nightengale-Lee's work challenges us to complicate our approaches to thinking and teaching about diversity in school settings.

References

Darling-Hammond, L. (2010). *The flat world and education: How America's commitment to equity will determine our future.* New York, NY: Teacher's College Press.

Grey, T. G., & Williams-Farrier, B. J. (2017). #Sippingtea: Two Black female literacy scholars sharing counter-stories to redefine our roles in the academy. *Journal of Literacy Research, 49*(4), 503–525.

Ladson-Billings, G. (2000). Fighting for our lives: Preparing teachers to teach African American students. *Journal of Teacher Education, 53*, 206–214.

Nieto, S. (2010). *Language, culture, and teaching: Critical perspectives.* New York, NY: Routledge.

Overstreet, M. (2019). My first year in academia or the mythical Black woman superhero takes on the ivory tower. *Journal of Women and Gender in Higher Education, 12*(1), 18–34.

CHAPTER 7

Approaching Educational Equity with White Preservice Teachers through an Intersectional Understanding of Self

Bianca Nightengale-Lee

Abstract

The racial, cultural, and linguistic, divide amid culturally and liguistically diverse (CLD) students and their White teachers is an important one. Research suggests that this "cultural dissonance" can result in a lack of knowledge and understanding, about diverse students, and how socio-historical forms of oppression can affect their achievement (Cross, 2005; Lazar, 2007; Grossman & McDonald, 2008). The goal of this work seeks to address this discord, by illuminating the link between critical pedagogy (Freire, 1970; hooks, 1994) and intersectionality (Crenshaw, 1989; Case, 2016), to support White teacher candidates (TCs) in analyzing privilege and oppression as it relates to themselves and their future students.

Initiating dialogue about power and privilege can be a challenging endeavor for White, middle-class TCs (Hall & Carlson, 2016). Blumenfeld and Jaekel note, that White novice educators may be hesitant to discuss issues related to social inequities, which include talking about how power and privilege impact the educational opportunities of some and not others. Socio-politically charged conversations often become more complex when facilitated by female faculty of color (FFOC) (Ladson-Billings, 1996). 20 years of examination reveal, that some White TCs employ defense based tactics such as *silence*, or *ambivalence* to disengage from topics of uncomfortability with FFOC (Ladson-Billings, 1996; McGowan, 2000; Stanley, 2006; Haddix, 2015). Thus this work delineates how a FFOC, utilized a critical-intersectional framework to circumvent the *silence* in a literacy methods course. Findings illustrate how this frame allowed space for White TCs to enact alternative identities beyond just race; cultivating open dialogue and honest reflection about privilege, power, and oppression.

Keywords

critical pedagogy – preservice teachers – intersectionality – culturally responsive pedagogy

1   **Introduction**

Critical theorist Paulo Freire (1970) placed emphasis on reading the word and the world as a means of emancipatory education. This outlook spoke to the importance of not only developing literal skills but inferential skills that position us to question the world, rather than simply exist within it. Similarly, literature across diversity & teacher education speak to the importance of developing preservice teachers' (PSTs) content knowledge alongside critical understandings of the world, to help them "understand the history of social and educational inequality, sociocultural differences, and the various processes by which inequities are maintained in schooling" (Kraehe & Brown, 2014, p. 171).

However, research shows initiating dialogue centered around unequal educational outcomes for diverse students can be a challenge for PSTs (Hall & Carlson, 2016). Blumenfeld and Jaekel (2012) note that approaching critical issues becomes convoluted when specifically working with White middle-class PSTs. The authors state that some White PSTs may be hesitant to discuss critical issues related to educational inequities, which include talking about how race, class, power, and privilege undermine the educational opportunities of students of color. Further, exploring weighty topics centered on privilege and oppression has proven even more challenging when facilitated by a female faculty of color (Ladson-Billings, 1996). Twenty years of examination reveal that some White PSTs employ resistance-based tactics such as silence or ambivalence to disengage from topics of uncomfortability with faculty of color (Stanley, 2006; Haddix, 2015). Though there is overwhelming literature that highlights the deficiencies of White PSTs in relation to their critical competence, relying on deficit conceptions alone is counterproductive in preparing them to question inequitable educational practices for students of color (Lowenstein, 2009; Nightengale-Lee, 2017). Therefore, new modes and methods of practice are needed to support White PSTs in understanding the impact of oppression on the educational trajectory of diverse students.

In this work, I share my experience as a Black female instructor exploring privilege and oppression with White PSTs in a literacy methods course. I begin by contextualizing the importance of developing critically competent PSTs in preparation for the needs of the ever-growing culturally and linguistically diverse (CLD) student population. I then reveal some of the pitfalls I experienced in broaching concepts of privilege and oppression with White PSTs, and how I used my mistakes to strengthen my practice. Finally, I explore how I used a critical-intersectional assignment to push White PSTs to question how systemic oppression may have shaped their educational outlook, and how these inequities may affect students of color.

From a broader perspective, this work seeks to consider what it might mean to approach critical issues of privilege and oppression through the lens of intersectional positionality. This outlook is grounded by the belief that to foster the level of critical consciousness necessary to challenge educational inequity, PSTs need preparation that acknowledges the societal constructs that shape education for students of color, and explicit instruction on the equitable practices that coincide with this approach. However, critical orientations such as these are immobilized if teacher educators do not provide the time and space for PSTs to first interrogate their own social positions in the world, and how these identities have shaped their experiences and beliefs about education (Ladson-Billings, 2007; Sleeter, 2008).

2   The Critical Divide

Finding effective strategies that support a critical agenda is a continual source of study in teacher education (Cochran-Smith, 2001; Collins, 2003; Ladson-Billings, 1994; Rose & Potts, 2011). The divide between White PSTs and their critical perspectives, point to an unchallenged mainstream ideology, situated in status quo interpretations of society. For many White PSTs, teacher education programs are their first introduction to critical conceptions of the world. Literature points to learning about candidates' perceptions, values, and beliefs as a primary step in aiding them to take an increased critical stance to teaching and learning. Acknowledging this, some teacher educators are beginning to infuse more critical methods of practice into their courses to help move White PSTs beyond shallow interpretations of educational inequity for students of color (Agnello, 2008; Lehman, 2017; Marx & Pecina, 2016; Miller & Mikulec, 2014).

Chubbuck (2010) argues that if teacher educators aim to foster critical commitments, they must first work to scaffold PST learning by acknowledging and affirming the value of their often-implicit knowledge and beliefs about teaching and schools (Neumann, 2013). Meaningful forms of White teacher candidate analysis require exploring their constructions of race, equity, and merit, which expose the ways in which they value and judge the world

(Howard, 2006; Rios & Lindley, 2004). Bridging the critical divide rests on the belief that critically conscious preparation will produce PSTs who question the practices, curriculum, and instructional decisions they make to better understand how these choices will affect the educational outcomes of students of color. Considering that the students PSTs will teach in the future will look, sound, or act differently than them, an introductory level of consciousness needs to be developed which first helps White PSTs understand themselves, their position in the world, and what this means as future educators.

3   Teaching with Eyes Wide Open

Using a critically oriented approach to teacher education, my work aims to provide avenues of agency, which support PSTs to enact forms of critical consciousness in their pedagogical practices. Upholding this stance, I have attempted to embed various forms of critical literacy into all of my classes. The lesson described in this chapter highlights a critical-intersectional assignment that I developed after reflecting on the feedback from my students in my methods classes within my first two semesters as an instructor. Prior to sharing the assignment itself, I deem it important to share the impetus upon which the lesson was created, as the experience has since shaped the way I view my practice, my students, and myself.

As a critical researcher, I entered the teacher education classroom with all the moxy and bravado of an ambitious yet naive scholar. My mind was armed with emancipatory thoughts of grandeur influenced by Mezirow's *Transformative Learning Theory* (Mezirow, 2000) and Freire's *Pedagogy of the Oppressed* (Freire, 1970), both my scholarly heroes. My goal was to teach literacy through a critical lens to lift the veil of societal blindness which prevented White PSTs from recognizing inequitable educational practice. Being well-versed in the teacher education literature on White PSTs, I knew they would be limited in their understanding of diversity, equity, and privilege. I was aggressive and persistent with my approach to equity education, and pushed White PSTs to confront systemic discrimination and racism in every class. Though well-intended this "pushing" provoked some of my White students to shut down and choose silence during critical discussion about equity and racism and discrimination. Those that didn't choose silence became emboldened in their resistance, and would display their disdain through questioning me in small and whole group settings. I can even recall one student asking me in a small group activity, "Why do we always have to talk about race?" I scolded this student for questioning me, and failed to fully justify her question with a response.

Though some students were reluctant to my approach, I walked away from the course feeling accomplished and justified in my work to unearth taken for granted perspectives in literacy education. I felt that my students were happy with the work that we'd done, and were thankful for my raw approach to equity, privilege, and oppression. However, after receiving my course evaluations, it became clear that my PSTs did not appreciate my approach to critical studies, as they revealed their disdain for my instruction through verbal assaults that called into question my validity as a literacy professor. This form of what I call, "evaluative backlash" caused me to have extremely low evaluation scores, which prompted my department chair to take notice. Responding to my chair's concerns, I highlighted the research and testimonies spanning 30 years that graphically recount the proverbial bumps and bruises of female faculty of color who endeavored to approach concepts of privilege and oppression with predominantly White PSTs (Baker-Bell, 2018; Collins, 2000; Delpit, 1995; Evans-Winters & Hoff, 2011; Jackson, 2016; Ladson-Billings, 1996). My chair seemed unaware of the literature on White racism and Black professors and seemed apathetic to my struggle. As a woman new to both the role of chair and to our university, she herself was facing many responsibilities and pressures that perhaps impeded her ability to see beyond the poor evaluations to the larger implications. Like other Black female scholars who have traversed these waters, I was angered by the students' negative backlash, and was even more disappointed by the lack of administrative support. Existing as Black female faculty in the predominately White and patriarchal parameters of academia was new for me and left me to question if carrying the burden of critical consciousness was worth the uncomfortable stares, side-eyes, and snapbacks that I received from students and colleagues.

Though this was a challenging time, it was also a pivotal point in my career because it allowed me to better understand the effects of White fragility (DiAngelo, 2011), and the defense-based tactics that some White PSTs used to avoid race-based conversation. Though recognizing the barriers that White PSTs may have addressing equity issues with a female faculty of color is important, dwelling in this reality was not helpful in closing the gap between what I wanted to teach my students, and what they were actually learning. I realized that I allowed my deficit-based assumptions about White PSTs to taint the way I engaged with them, by devaluing their perspectives, which in turn silenced their voice in the classroom. Thus, I had to take a step back and reflect on my instructional practices and curriculum to rethink the way I approached teaching critical issues. This kind of introspection was "soul work" for me because it required me to take an unfiltered view of my intentions to discern if they matched my practice. What I discovered through my reflection was that I was missing a key component to discussing privilege and oppression with White PSTs. I realized that I was failing to connect privilege and oppression to the lives of the White PSTs I taught. The theme that I noticed in the evaluative backlash was that many students felt a disconnect from what I was teaching them about students of color and themselves. Accepting this, I began to shift my approach to educational inequity by helping PSTs better understand their own privileged and oppressed identities within society through intersectional positionality analysis.

4 An Intersectional View of White Preservice Teachers

Though one could argue that the modifications I made to ease White PSTs into critical conversation perpetuate the racial and social insulation of White Fragility, recent literature in intersectional studies and teacher education (Grant & Zwier, 2016; Case, 2013) suggest that foundational steps in equity awareness initiates helping PSTs to "not only have an understanding for the diverse populations with whom they will work, but also foster the same within themselves" (Miller & Mikulec, 2014, p. 19). Most traditional methods aimed to strengthen self-awareness narrow the notion of "self" into a singular perspective, which examine race, class, or gender as separate identities. However, some teacher educators are challenging mono-identity approaches to self-awareness and adopting intersectional frameworks that provide a clearer picture of how multiple identities work together to shape our understanding of who we are and how we experience the world.

Due to the lack of critically infused curricula and practices in k-12 settings, many PSTs are uninformed of the socio-historical context in which learning is situated. Unaware of this, some PSTs are oblivious of how learning is negotiated through intersectional identities, which provide the lenses from which students make sense of text, and henceforth make sense of their world (McCormick, 1996). The primary theme of intersectionality examines "the experiences and struggles of disenfranchised groups to broaden and deepen understandings of human life and behavior" (Collins & Bilge, 2016, p. 36). I argue that intersectionality lays the foundation for critical conversations centered on equity by enabling PSTs to identify the duality of their own identity as being both privileged and oppressed (Williamson, 2013). This perspective allows PSTs to realistically situate themselves in the world and counter reductionist-based notions that rely only on race and gender to define identity. This level of self-awareness is foundational in helping to acquire the consciousness necessary to access, acknowledge, and accept critical conceptions of the world (Grant & Sleeter, 2007).

In a literacy context, broadening PSTs' understanding of alternative social identities through intersectionality can act both as a mirror and a door. This mode of social analysis acts as a mirror from which PSTs can locate themselves as simultaneously privileged and oppressed, and provide a door to open conversations about how these divergent social locations position them as literate beings. Williamson states, "by taking up the idea that literacy is socially constructed and that our identities as literate people are dependent on who we are and in what contexts, candidates begin to challenge their assumptions about what it means to be literate and how literacy develops" (2013, p. 140). Potentially this lens allows PSTs to challenge traditional conceptions of literacy learning, enabling them to understand and relate to students of color by acknowledging the social categories, which may influence their literacy development and educational outlook.

5 Critical-Intersectional Assignment

Though ideologies which undergird critical pedagogy predicate on fighting injustice and challenging oppression, translation of these abstract concepts unearths a unique tension as teacher educators look to transform theory into practice. The assignment described here derives from my work as literacy instructor, where I aimed to marry theory with practice through a critical-intersectional approach. This assignment was used in a literacy methods course that met once a week for three hours. The institution in which I worked established a unique partnership with the local school district, where professional and methods courses were taught within designated high-needs schools. This model aimed to provide an authentic learning experience, reflective of the growing student population regionally as well as nationally. The PSTs that I worked with were in their second literacy methods course, and were a year and a half away from starting their student teaching. The majority of the PSTs who engaged in this assignment were White and female, with the exception of one White male. Though all the PSTs identified as White, their socioeconomic backgrounds and educational histories varied greatly, which I discovered through this assignment.

To set the stage to explore critical issues in literacy education, I implemented this assignment in the first two weeks of the semester. This lesson was used as the platform from which critical conversations were initiated, and was foundational to broader discussion centered on privilege, oppression and educational outcomes. I begin the lesson by introducing the concept of intersectional positionality by sharing the textbook definition, and provided each with the Matrix of Oppression (Collins, 1991).

The matrix of oppression was a good visual that helped PSTs understand how various intersectional identities position us as oppressed or privileged based on socially accepted definitions of dominant norms. From here, I put the focus on myself and shared with them my intersectional positionality, as multi-oppressed and multi-privileged, based on the matrix of oppression. As a class we then compare my intersectional identities to that of a famous, rich, white male politician; I highlight for this activity that the politician and I are more than just our race, gender, and class. I ask the students to consider how our intersectional identities have shaped our life experiences. Specifically for this exercise, I showed a picture of the politician and myself with a list of all of the social identity markers. As a class we explored each marker and identified who was more privileged and oppressed and how these identities overlapped to create our experiences.

From here we begin to discuss the idea of social privilege and how people can be privileged or oppressed beyond just skin color, as well as the implications of these social categories on our educational outlook. To help connect intersectionality to student outcomes, I shared with PSTs that I was labeled with a learning disability by age 6. Based on the matrix, ableism is an oppressed identity. Revealing this opens the conversation to explore how society views students with disabilities and the negative effects that labels can have on students' educational achievement.

I then turn the focus on the PSTs themselves and ask them to reflect on their own identities within the Matrix of Oppression. Using the Matrix as a guide I asked them to color the identities that were most important to them and of which they are most aware. Once this was completed I asked students to share with the class their thoughts about their identities as both oppressed and privileged. Finally, I ask student to write a short reflection about one privileged and one oppressed identity that shaped their educational experience. After reviewing each PSTs' reflection at home, I begin the next class talking again about their multiple identities and their educational experience. Making the time for PSTs to honor their identities opened the door for deeper conversation in my classroom, where students were connecting with each other and me based on their various identities.

The next step was to then take their understanding of intersectional identities and think about how these identities affect students from diverse cultural, social, linguistic, and economic backgrounds. I supported students in this analysis by providing small groups with fictitious student vignettes, which provided the student's name, face, and 7 of their intersectional identities. In small groups students had to create posters identifying how many of the students' identities were privileged/oppressed, and how these identities may have framed the way the student viewed the world. After creating their posters, PSTs had to present their findings to the class. An example of one of the student vignettes is illustrated in Figure 7.1.

The intersectional identity assignment took a total of three hours to complete in class and, though time was always limited, I found this strategy beneficial. Specifically, I noticed that once students began looking at privilege and oppression through the lens of intersectionality, they became more willing to engage in thinking and discussing critical issues focused on educational equity in the methods classroom. For me, this introductory approach to privilege and oppression was helpful in circumventing the silence that usually exists when discussing equity in literacy education. Since this method is in its infancy I will continue to modify and adjust the approach based on the needs of the PSTs I teach. I look forward to exploring new ways of utilizing intersectionality to help student analyze and critique equitable educational practice.

- ❖ **Ethnicity:** Somali
- ❖ **Social Class:** Lower class
- ❖ **Religion:** Islam (Muslim)
- ❖ **Language:** Maay Maay & some English
- ❖ **Country of Origin:** Somalia
- ❖ **Gender:** Female
- ❖ **Ability:** Above Average Cognition
- ❖ **Area of Residence:** Rural Area

➤ *How many identities are privileged?*
➤ *How many are oppressed?*
➤ *How do these identities frame the way this student views the world?*

FIGURE 7.1   Bashira

6   Implications of This Work

6.1   *Curricular*
While literature surrounds effective modes of social justice teacher education, this exploration furthers the conversation by examining preservice teachers'

intersectional identities and the role they play in sculpting curricula that reflect not only their instructional needs, but their emotional and social needs as well. Considering research which suggests that some White PSTs resist multicultural frameworks due to White shame, cultural misunderstanding, and ethnocentrism, critical-intersectional assignments such as this work to broaden PSTs cultural lens to better understand how their social locations in society position them as privileged or oppressed beings. Teacher educators may look to a critical-intersectional approach to curriculum development to help PSTs adopt a more intersectional outlook which may provide a more student reflective and critical approach to instructional practice (Scrimgeour & Ovsienko, 2015). Being that this work is exploratory in nature, more activities like it need to be tried in various contexts and settings to better understand the role it plays in supporting PSTs' self-awareness, which may inform larger conversation around curricular design elements relative to critical practices.

6.2 *Teacher Educator*

Keeping it real with yourself is not always an easy practice, especially if your goals are well intended. However, I believe that teacher educators who are committed to promoting a critical stance must "simultaneously be critically thinking about and inquiring into their own practices" (Scherff & Singer, 2012, p. 264) and how these practices shape the learning outcomes of their students. Taking on a critical practitioner stance required a high level of inquiry, reflectivity, and reflexivity to continuously raise new questions about myself and my pedagogy. It is important that as we approach the subject of criticality in teacher education, we hold a critical awareness about the varying positionalities of our students and how their life experiences influence their societal outlooks. For example, we cannot presume to know all of the experiences of White PSTs by simply acknowledging their race alone. This form of overgeneralization is dangerous because it fails to capture the dynamic identities that comprise their lived experiences. Freire (1970) articulates this point further by stating, "Many educational plans have failed because their authors designed them according to their own personal views of reality, never once taking into account to whom the program was ostensibly directed" (p. 75). More plainly, appreciating, acknowledging, and understanding how PSTs' intersectional identities have shaped their lived experiences can help teacher educators understand how to reach and teach PSTs about critical topics in teacher education.

By first committing to honoring PSTs' intersectional identities, teacher educators can begin to approach inequitable practices based on systemic racism, discrimination, and marginalization more seamlessly with White PSTs. Approaching these kind of weighty educational issues are paramount if we want to prepare PSTs with the skills to successfully meet the needs of students of color (Giroux, 2004). Teacher educators have opportunities to engage PSTs in activities specifically designed to increase cultural awareness of inequitable educational practices and recognize opportunities to promote criticality. However, efforts to enact criticality into any course will falter if teacher educators are not willing to take critical stances in their classroom practice. Maintaining a critical posture to teacher education must start with self-reflection to ensure that instructional methods and curriculum are reflective of the needs of students of color as well the socio-emotional aptitude of the PSTs that we teach.

Each semester I have listened, leveraged, and learned from PSTs about the methods which have best suited their understanding of critical literacy. In a methods course, embedding elements of equity, diversity, and difference alongside concrete methodological practice is a delicate dance. Every class, every student, and every course evaluation has become a navigational compass used to gauge if I got the dance right, or if I needed to re-work my steps. Though the methods to revise and refine effective strategies which promote critical literacy are "messy," they are necessary as we aim to prepare the next generation of educators for the realities of 21st century contexts.

References

Agnello, M. F. (2008). Freirean cultural lenses for promoting future teacher literacy knowledge. *Journal of Thought, 43*(2), 107–130.

Baker-Bell, A. (2017). For Loretta: A black woman literacy scholar's journey to prioritizing self-preservation and black feminist womanist storytelling. *Journal of Literacy Research, 49*(4), 526–543.

Blumenfeld, W. J., & Jaekel, K. (2012). Exploring levels of Christian privilege awareness among preservice teachers. *Journal of Social Issues, 68*(1), 128–144.

Case, K. (2013). *Deconstructing privilege: Teaching and learning as allies in the classroom.* New York, NY: Routledge.

Chubbuck, S. M. (2010). Individual and structural orientations in socially just teaching: Conceptualization, implementation, and collaborative effort. *Journal of Teacher Education, 61*(3), 197–210.

Cochran-Smith, M. (2001). The outcomes question in teacher education. *Teaching and Teacher Education, 17*(5), 527–546.

Collins, P. H. (2000). *Black feminist thought: Knowledge, consciousness and the politics of empowerment* (2nd ed.). New York, NY: Routledge.

Collins, P. H., & Bilge, S. (2016). *Intersectionality.* Hoboken, NJ: John Wiley & Sons.

Crenshaw, K. (1991). Mapping the margins: Intersectionality, identity politics, and violence against women of color. *Stanford Law Review, 43*(6), 1241–1299.

Delpit, L. (2005). *The politics of curricular change: Race, hegemony, and power in education.* New York, NY: Peter Lang.

DiAngelo, R. (2011). White fragility. *The International Journal of Critical Pedagogy, 3*(3), 54–70.

Evans-Winters, V. E., & Twyman Hoff, P. (2011). The aesthetics of white racism in pre-service teacher education: A critical race theory perspective. *Race Ethnicity and Education, 14*(4), 461–479.

Freire, P. (1970). *Pedagogy of the oppressed.* New York, NY: Bloomsbury Publishing.

Giroux, H. A. (2004). Critical pedagogy and the postmodern/modern divide: Towards a pedagogy of democratization. *Teacher Education Quarterly, 31*(1), 31–47.

Grant, C. A., & Sleeter, C. E. (2011). *Doing multicultural education for achievement and equity.* New York, NY: Routledge.

Grant, C. A., & Zwier, E. (2011). Intersectionality and student outcomes: Sharpening the struggle against racism, sexism, classism, ableism, heterosexism, nationalism, and linguistic, religious, and geographical discrimination in teaching and learning. *Multicultural Perspectives, 13*(4), 181–188.

Haddix, M. (2015). *Cultivating racial and linguistic diversity in literacy teacher education: Teachers like me.* New York, NY: Routledge.

Hall, J. M., & Carlson, K. (2016). Marginalization: A revisitation with integration of scholarship on globalization, intersectionality, privilege, microaggressions, and implicit biases. *Advances in Nursing Science, 39*(3), 200–215.

Hill Collins, P. (2010). The new politics of community. *American Sociological Review, 75*(1), 7–30.

Hill-Collins, P., & Bilge, S. (2016). *Intersectionality.* Hoboken, NJ: John Wiley & Sons.

Howard, G. R. (2006). *We can't teach what we don't know: White teachers, multiracial schools.* New York, NY: Teachers College Press.

Jackson, T. O. (2015). Perspectives and insights of preservice teachers of color on developing culturally responsive pedagogy at predominantly white institutions. *Action in Teacher Education, 37*(3), 223–237.

Kraehe, A. M., & Brown, K. D. (2014). Intersectional imagination: Arts-based strategies for teaching critical sociocultural knowledge. In C. A. Grant & E. Zwier (Eds.), *Intersectionality and urban education: Identities, policies, spaces & power* (pp. 171–191.) Charlotte, NC: Information Age Publishing.

Ladson-Billings, G. (1995). Toward a theory of cultural relevant pedagogy. *American Educational Research Journal, 32*(3), 465–491.

Ladson-Billings, G. (2007). Pushing past the achievement gap: An essay on the language of deficit. *The Journal of Negro Education, 76*(3), 316–323.

Ladson-Billings, G., & Tate, W. F. (1995). Toward a critical race theory of education. *Teachers College Record, 97*(1), 47–68.

Lehman, C. L. (2017). Multicultural competence: A literature review supporting focused training for preservice teachers teaching diverse students. *Journal of Education and Practice, 8*(10), 109–116.

Lowenstein, K. L. (2009). The work of multicultural teacher education: Reconceptualizing white teacher candidates as learners. *Review of Educational Research, 79,* 163–196.

Marx, D., & Pecina, U. (2016). Community: The missing piece in preparing teacher candidates for future urban classrooms. *Action in Teacher Education, 38*(4), 344–357.

Mezirow, J. (2000). *Learning as transformation: Critical perspectives on a theory in progress.* San Francisco, CA: Jossey-Bass.

Miller, P. C., & Mikulec, E. A. (2014). Pre-service teachers confronting issues of diversity through a radical field experience. *Multicultural Education, 21*(2), 18–24.

Neumann, J. W. (2013). Critical pedagogy's problem with changing teachers' disposition towards critical teaching. *Interchange, 44*(1–2), 129–147.

Nightengale-Lee, B. (2017). *Educating critically: challenging the familiar contours of literacy teacher education* (Doctoral dissertation). University of Louisville, Louisville KY.

Rios, F., & Lindley, L. (2004). Taking stands for social justice. *Scholar-Practitioner Quarterly, 2*(2), 89–106.

Rose, D. G., & Potts, A. D. (2011). Examining teacher candidate resistance to diversity: What can teacher educators learn? *International Journal of Multicultural Education, 13*(2), 1–19.

Scherff, L., & Singer, N. R. (2012). The preservice teachers are watching: Framing and reframing the field experience. *Teaching and Teacher Education, 28*(2), 263–272.

Scrimgeour, M., & Ovsienko, H. (2015). Anti-racism pedagogy in pre-service teacher education: The role of intersectional privilege studies. *The Journal of Educational Enquiry, 14*(2).

Sleeter, C. E. (2001). Preparing teachers for culturally diverse schools: Research and the overwhelming presence of whiteness. *Journal of Teacher Education, 52*(2), 94–106.

Stanley, C. A. (2006). Coloring the academic landscape: Faculty of color breaking the silence in predominantly White colleges and universities. *American Educational Research Journal, 43*(4), 701–736.

Williamson, P. (2013). Engaging literacy practices through inquiry and enactment in teacher education. In C. Kosnik, J. Rowsell, P. Williamson, R. Simon, & C. Beck (Eds.), *Literacy teacher educators: Preparing teachers for a changing world* (pp. 135–147). Dordrecht, The Netherlands: Sense Publishers.

BRIDGING THE THEME

Reflective Action Matters

Mikkaka Overstreet and Lori Norton-Meier

Teaching is an art form that a practitioner refines throughout their career. To do so, that teacher must reflect on their instruction, their students' progress, and the needs and strengths of their contexts. A good teacher must be reflective because only through constant reflection can there be continued growth. Reflection alone, however, is not enough. Reflection without action is much like wishing without effort. Growth and change cannot come about without action. In the previous chapter, Bianca Nightengale-Lee guided us through her efforts to push her preservice teachers (PSTs) to be more reflective about their own intersectional identities and those of K-12 students. In the following chapter, Emily Zuccaro considers how this reflection becomes active: how does the reflective work impact PSTs thoughts, beliefs, and values and how, in turn, does that affect how they talk about children?

CHAPTER 8

Positioning Students as Writers: A Discourse Analysis in Teacher Education

Emily Zuccaro

Abstract

Through a university-community partnership, students at a Southeast Central university met once a week for a clinical writing methods course at an elementary school. The writing methods course is one of their first classes in the teacher preparation program and afforded students the opportunity to develop a one-on-one teaching relationship with students in a second-grade classroom. University students supported second-grade students in creating digital stories and recorded observational data through the semester, later discussing these observations with classmates. This chapter uses discourse analysis as an analytic tool to uncover how preservice teachers initially position children as objects of affection to powerful writers and its implications for future clinical method partnerships.

Keywords

writing instruction – preservice teachers – figured worlds – positioning children

1 Introduction

Various teacher education models and configurations are enacted at universities across the United States, yet Zeichner and Bier (2012) explain, "There is widespread agreement in the U.S. that providing high quality clinical experiences to teacher candidates is the key element in providing effective teacher preparation" (p. 165). Growing scholarship attests "that much of what teachers need to learn must be learned in and from practice rather than in preparing for practice" (Ball & Cohen, 1999; Hammerness, Darling-Hammond, & Bransford, 2005, as cited in Zeichner, 2010). At the university where I work, preservice teachers attended classes at local elementary, middle, and high schools in order to learn from university faculty and practicing teachers at the school. Additionally, the university offered preservice teachers (PSTS) a multitude of support structures, such as their classes that take place on campus, their field placement hours in which they are required to meet a certain number of hours inside classrooms watching instructional practices, and student teaching, for example. This collection of experiences constituted their professional training as they shifted paradigms from students to teachers, while living in between both worlds in the education field.

University students may face periods of disequilibrium as their ideologies, knowledge, beliefs, and values about teaching and learning are renegotiated, contested, reinscribed and more through their schooling. This disequilibrium can be a consequence of competing discourses from various figured worlds that PSTS have constructed and participated in, as well as the ones that they are expected to enter as they choose teaching as a profession. Clinical method students face an even more unique disequilibrium, as the figured worlds of the university and the figured worlds of the school may be in competition as well. Our understanding of such worlds can help us better prepare our students as we gain our understanding from their language-in-use as they describe the events that constitute their experiences in school.

In this chapter, I examine and answer the following research questions:
- How are preservice educators' knowledge, beliefs, and values reflected in their language?
- How—if at all—do these knowledge, beliefs, and values change over time in positioning children in a certain way?

2 Context

The following data were collected from a cohort of first-semester preservice elementary teachers in a clinical writing methods class. PSTS met once a week for six hours at a local elementary school for three hours for my writing methods course and three hours for a learning community/classroom management course. The university created a signature partnership initiative with local schools at the elementary, middle, and high school level to address disparities in an impoverished part of the city. We (the university) collaborated with a second-grade classroom and once a week, PSTS watched as I taught a mini-lesson to the second-grade students, then they spent the remaining time working with a second-grade buddy. PSTS benefitted from attending class at the elementary school as it afforded them time to confer with a student and practice the methods they learned in class every week.

As it was their first semester in the program, most PSTs had limited experience with lesson planning, implementation, and instructional time with school-aged children. Some PSTs told me they tutored children or worked in an after-school camp, while one PST had worked as an instructional assistant at another school in the district. However, most PSTs explained they had not worked with students in this sort of setting with explicit instruction in writing methods. Their first semester in the education college constituted methods courses, content courses, and fieldwork. PSTs' fieldwork assignment placed them in the same elementary school for an entire instructional day outside of our own class time. The collection of coursework and fieldwork offered PSTs support and resources to draw upon as they started to work with children in a more professional context.

The PSTs' own K-12 writing education and their conceptualization of what constitutes school and "good" writing reflects beliefs and knowledge constructed in figured worlds. Much research has contributed to the scholarship on figured worlds, which helped us understand our PSTs' language and their knowledge, beliefs, and values. Marsh and Lammers (2011) offered their explanation of figured worlds as "the beliefs, values, and attitudes held that inform what we say and how we act, read, and interact" (p. 97). Figured world research provided understanding to the ways in which knowledge, beliefs, and values were enacted in teacher education in several ways. The shifting professional identity between student and teacher involved the learning of new acts, working toward certain outcomes, understanding the larger and grander discourses, and encountering new characters and actors along the way. This also included how preservice teachers positioned children in their new identity as teacher, where talking about children and their learning was newly configured as they assumed a teacher identity. Most PSTs explained that for most of their schooling, they were given prompts to which they were expected to respond. They explained that they were evaluated based on the mechanics of writing versus the content and ideas of their writing. In my class, the PSTs spent time examining how to create a writing workshop that values students' ideas over mechanics, which proved challenging for some of them. For example, many PSTs expressed their concern over a student who isn't spelling things correctly, that what their student is writing "isn't what the assignment is," or that they have a number of run-on sentences. We spent much time trying to unpack the way they had experienced writing and the ways they were implementing the course methods with their partners.

3 Methods

There were 10 women and 1 man in my methods course. Most were traditional college-aged students; however, there were a couple of PSTs who switched majors or left school for a semester so there was a wider range in student ages in my class. My PSTs specialized in various areas such as special education, social studies, early childhood, and math. University students met with their second-grade partner(s) every week for a total of seven to eight meetings. I asked my PSTs to fill out a responsive teaching cycle sheet during and after each meeting. This document required students to record their observations with students, expand their interpretations of the conference, and plan next steps for the following session with their partner. I allowed PSTs time to fill out each section with as much detail as they could, and followed with a group and class discussion to unpack any productive stories or inquiries into their work with their partners. There were three groups: two groups of four and one group of three students. Data were collected from each group discussion after this time and most discussions lasted about ten minutes each as PSTs discussed their time with their students.

The data analyzed below were from two groups of girls in my class. I analyzed two groups on February 6th, and one group on March 20th. Paulina, Abigail, Michelle, and Miranda sat in one group, with Louise, Bethany, and Viktoria in the other. I included two groups in the first analysis because the PSTs chose different seating arrangements later in the semester, where Viktoria had taken Miranda's seat. In order to account for and demonstrate the ways in which Viktoria's linguistic forms, utterances, cultural models and more moved (or did not move) across events, I felt it necessary to include her even though she was initially sitting with a different group.

3.1 *Researcher's Reflexivity*

As a researcher, it was important to include my reflexivity as part of the data collection and analysis. I needed to consider several things as I moved forward in this process. First, this was the first time I taught a university-level course by myself. At the same time, I was taking a course about classroom discourse analysis. The timing of both events was important to note, as I believed the coursework elevated my awareness of my speech with my students and at times, it may have been more "monitored" than normal. Secondly, I believed I am more likely to paint my students in a more positive light than critical because as their instructor, I believe I am inclined to protect or defend them as they make their way through their coursework and field experiences to become a classroom teacher. My subjectivity influenced my subsequent analysis, as a result of knowing the participants well. I recognize I am supposed to challenge them as their instructor but I also felt as they are in their first semester, they needed more support than challenges in synthesizing coursework and readings and making decisions regarding their work with children.

4 Analysis

I combined two approaches to discourse analysis for my data. I analyzed my data using guidelines from Wortham and Reyes (2015) and Fairclough (1989) in order to understand how the text features of their speech reflected their knowledge, beliefs, and values, as well as understanding the ways in which their figured worlds evolved over time. I outlined this approach in the following sections.

4.1 *Discourse Analysis beyond the Speech Event*

Using discourse analysis across the speech event as an analytic strategy provides researchers with tools for examining the social action accomplished through multiple, linked discursive events and the consequences for learning and socialization identities in classrooms today. Wortham and Reyes (2015) draw on the field of linguistic anthropology for their discourse analysis approach. Their approach studies the ways in which "linguistic forms, utterances, cultural models, individuals and groups travel across events" (p. 1). They argue that discourse analysis is only useful when studied across events because processes like learning and socialization affects the individual's behavior as they advance through and live out multiple events.

Discourse analysis across the speech event entails multiple phases of analysis that begin with mapping narrated events, which is the content of the talk. The next phase consists of three processes which are dialectical in nature and involve establishing relevant context through the use of indexicals, which are signs that point to their object. Wortham and Reyes (2015) explain, "Relevant context gets established as speakers organize their messages systematically … to foreground certain aspects, and as other speakers subsequently presuppose the same aspects of the context" (p. 11). The first step, selecting indexicals, involves ascertaining signs that could point to certain types of social action which assists in establishing the relevant context such as deictics and reported speech. Deictics are "words or expressions such as *this* or *that* which stand in for prior or future discourse, or refer exophorically to objects in the context" (p. 48). To refer to something exophorically is to refer to something outside of the text, such as "Did you get those?" to which *those* was uttered previously.

Reported speech is used to describe speech that took place at some other time, such as "Well, he said it was really important to write her an email." The next step, construing indexicals, relies on the metapragmatic processes, or understanding the ways in which language performs actions. The analyst infers based on things such as voicing and positioning. The final step involving indexicals is describing how these signs become more stable in nature and establish relevant context and signal social action. The last phase attempts to interpret the social action occurring over events.

4.2   Fairclough and Critical Discourse Analysis

Fairclough (1989) established his approach to discourse analysis through what is known as Critical Discourse Analysis (CDA). He states, "Language is a part of society ... there is an internal and dialectical relationship between language and society" (p. 23). Fairclough defines texts as both oral and written and that they are a product and part of social interaction. Discourse analysis, in his approach, entails the productive and interpretive analysis of the interplay between text properties and 'member resources,' or the "peoples' knowledge of language, representations of the natural and social world they inhabit, values, beliefs, assumptions, and so on" (p. 24). These resources are socially generated, and Fairclough claims they are also unequally distributed. People draw upon what is available and use such available resources for engaging in social practices.

Fairclough provides guidelines for analyzing text features, explaining that such features can be "regarded as particular choices from among the options ... available in the discourse types which the text draws upon" (p. 110). Fairclough defines three values to features of a text: experiential, relational, and expressive. He explains that a feature with experiential value has "a trace and a cue to the way in which the text producer's experience of the natural or social world is represented" (p. 112). He explains further that experiential value reflects the knowledge and beliefs of the text producer. Fairclough establishes a set of questions to guide analysis through the different text values. I believe this particular analytic strategy illuminates my PSTs' current beliefs and knowledge about children as writers, as I draw upon the following questions for my analysis:
1. What experiential values do words have?
    – Is there rewording or overwording?
2. What experiential values do grammatical features have?
    – Is agency unclear?
    – Are sentences active or passive?
    – Are sentences positive or negative?

I situated the combination of Fairclough's CDA and figured worlds in a linguistic anthropology discourse across speech events approach to account for what Fairclough mentions above: an analysis of the text features and the member resources available. I believe it is important for us to analyze the features and resources of the PSTs over time, as Wortham and Reyes encourage us, as to understand the impact of the events like the methods class and other influences in the PSTs' professional training and education and the PSTs' following behavior in positioning children as writers.

4.3 Transcription

I used Gee (1991) and his linguistic narrative transcription as my method of organizing the transcripts. He explains that he "uses the organization of discourse to manipulate images or themes rooted in the life world or world view of the person using the language" (Gee, 1990, as cited in Gee, 1991). This method of transcription allowed me to see how the PSTs discuss and position their work inside school and with children and the lifeworlds in which they are situated.

5 Findings

In this chapter, I analyzed the data using Fairclough's guidelines of rewording (such as paraphrasing) and overwording (using many words which are similar in nature, perhaps to get a point across). Rewording or overwording is accomplished through the use of synonyms, antonyms, and hyponyms. Hyponyms were specific instances of a more general word, known as hypernyms. For example, a hypernym is "color" and its hyponym is "blue." Additionally, I examined agency and the use of active, passive, positive, and negative sentences. I embed Wortham and Reyes' approach within each section as well. The transcripts are found in the appendices for additional context, and I included several key lines for demonstrating such occurrences.

5.1 Rewording and Overwording

5.1.1 February 6th

In this first episode, students discussed their first meeting with their second-grade partners in which they created a heart map. The heart map was a prewriting engagement as part of a larger unit of study in the writing methods course I was teaching. Overwording was evident as Abigail employed reported speech in line 39, describing what students say about their teacher ("They're like 'I wanna buy Ms. Lewandowski a new outfit'"). Viktoria used reported speech on line 48 ("He said the hardest thing about being a writer is that he doesn't have enough time to write"). Michelle also used overwording in lines 3–14, describing her student and his friendship with another boy. Paulina reworded affect words through synonyms such as cute (lines 18 and 24) and sweet (lines 13 and 29). Michelle positioned drawing in opposition to or an antonym of writing in lines 15–17, which can actually be considered a hyponym (drawing can be considered an instance of writing, in this case).

> 15. um he was a lot more focused on drawing than actually writing
>
> 16. so it was really hard to get him to like/want to write
>
> 17. cuz he wanted/to draw everything (Mic)

This reflected her belief that drawing and writing are separate processes. She also named "everything" in line 3 and gives specific instances of it "motorcycles" and "best friend." Viktoria reworded a more generic term, "interesting" in line 44 to provide an instance (hyponym) of what she means by interesting in line 45, "they're both at … different sides." This reflected the ways in which she valued a diversity within her students' writing.

5.1.2   March 20th

In this later episode, PSTs drafted a personal narrative with their second-grade partner for a couple of weeks and discussed their writing. Notably, their rewording and synonym use evolved from affect evaluative words to achievement evaluative words. Paulina employed "insanely advanced" (line 75), "part of the gifted and talented" (line 101) and "really really smart" in line 76. Abigail said, "Wow, she's smart" in line 82 and Michelle followed up with "Wow that's good" (line 84). Viktoria used rewording in the forms of antonyms in line 134 when she said, "So I was like you don't want to draw/you don't want to add words." Paulina used a hypernym "good" in line 86 and provides hyponyms, or specific instance of it in lines 87–88 when she said, "She's really good at what she does." Good can be equated with good writer, as Paulina explained she "organize papers, laid them out, put paper in order" to provide specific instances of it. Her adjectives evolved from "cute" and "sweet" to "smart," "advanced," and "good" over speech events. I discuss this occurrence in more detail in a subsequent section.

Overwording through reported speech was evident in many places in the episode such as:

POSITIONING STUDENTS AS WRITERS

1. line 79 "so she said, 'Mr. Kurtzman called *us* to the carpet'"
2. line 94 "and he said, 'Yes, she's like extremely good'"
3. line 110 "he was like, 'I don't want to do it/I hate my life/Don't ask me to do anything cuz I'm not/I hate writing"
4. line 117 "I was like 'Oh, put these together;'"
5. line 121 "I basically wrote, 'these are the parts of your story'"
6. lines 123–124 "I was like, 'No this is not your story/this is your outline'"
7. line 133 "but he was like 'I don't want to draw anymore'"
8. lines 140–152 (shown below)

   140. Be like "So what happened?"/and just let him talk about it

   141. because maybe he doesn't want to like/he won't see it as work that way

   142. Be like "Yeah but what happened?"/and then be like/"Oh, well do you want to include that in your story?" (P)

   143. Well I've tried that/like I have/"Tell me your story/what happened"

   144. and he was like/"nothing/the car was broken"

   145. and I was like/"How did it break?"

   146. He's like "I don't know"

   147. I was like "Something's wrong with it"/and he said "The engine"

   148. and I was like/"Oh what happened to the engine?/How long was it broken?"

   149. I tried asking him questions and/"What happened before that?/Who fixed the car?" (V)

   150. Or maybe even encourage him/say

   151. "Well do you want to write about something that you know a little more about?"

   152. Like something happier/a fun story you WANT to talk about?"

Overwording was seen here through reported speech as Viktoria and Paulina narrated and repeated student and teacher talk to illustrate a point. This process elaborated narrated events and helped us understand the social action at hand. Preservice educators frequently relied on reported speech in their efforts to describe what took place with their students in each episode. Overwording can be a method for characterizing students which can lead to particular social actions. Viktoria's reported speech and the reported speech of her classmates characterized her second-grade partner as a reluctant writer, one that would never finish a story. The social action that follows could be one of many, including attempts to motivate or encourage the student, or deciding not to do anything because there was nothing left to do for this particular student.

5.2 *Agency, Passive, and Active Sentences*

5.2.1 February 6th

In this first episode, Viktoria discussed her two second-grade partners, noting the difference between the two but expressing excitement about working with them. Notably, she used active sentences for her student, Ezekiel. She said in line 47, "He likes to write because he can write his feelings down." In line 11, Michelle used active sentences about how her buddy wrote on his heart map. Her language reflected her desire to limit his agency in line 16 as she said it was hard to get him to want to write. Paulina used active sentences to reflect what her student did "She'd mention it and then she'd write it down" (line 23). PSTs mostly commented on what their second-grade partners did, with brief or little reflection on what action they themselves took during this time. This could be due to the fact it was the first meeting and second graders were brainstorming writing topics from their lives, an engagement that did not require much facilitation from my PSTs at this time.

5.2.2 March 20th

In this later episode, agency was complicated by PSTs and their reflection of their work with their students. Viktoria reflected on a perceived challenging moment with one of her students. She expressed her actions in limiting her student's agency, in line 106 when she said, "I told him he can't change [his story] anymore." Her student voiced his agency in line 110, when he said, "I don't want to [work on my story today]" and in line 133 when he said, "I don't want to draw anymore." Viktoria pushed back on her student in lines 123–124 when she explained after she modeled writing, "he was trying to copy my sentence and I was like no." At times, she only reflected on his decisions (in line 117, she said, "he said he doesn't want [combine parts of his story]").

Abigail positioned her student in control of his writing when she said in line 67, "He has a lot of trouble with spelling," placing him as the subject and able to move in his writing, instead of positioning him as being the "victim" of spelling and the object of spelling's hold. A noteworthy observation involved the use of "to be" verbs, like "was" or "were" that indicate passive voice. In lines 70, the use of "was writing" and line 99 "was using" in their speech did not necessarily constitute passive sentence use because the student was still the subject instead of the object. Instead, this reflects the past tense of the event.

Noteworthy was the evolution of student rewording through the use of synonyms to describe their second-grade partner. Students' language on February 6th contained much affective language, positioning children as objects of affective evaluation through words like "cute" and "sweet." Clancy (1999) states that cute is a key "affect word" (as cited in Burdelski, 2010, p. 66). According to Ochs (1992), language directly indexes affective stance through "affect specifiers," such as lexicon, pragmatic particles, and diminutive markers, and "affect intensifiers," like repetition and reduplication, phonological lengthening, and quantifiers, which in turn can indirectly index gender (as cited in Burdelski, 2010, p. 68). Wortham and Reyes (2015) explain evaluative indexicals such as labels like *cute* and *sweet* "point to relevant context in ways that potentially characterize and evaluate narrated characters and narrating participants" (p. 51). Second graders are initially characterized through affect words by PSTs, which could reflect the ways in which their figured worlds are those of children as objects of affection, where what they do is characterized under the auspices of childhood, innocence, and naiveté.

5.3 *Positive and Negative Framing*
5.3.1 February 6th

In this episode, positive framing is enacted in lines 21 when Paulina, in describing her second-grade partner said, "everything was still focused on [our work together]." She continued later in line 25 to say, "I felt like kids really respected Mr. Kurtzman and listened to him." Abigail contributed her perspective by saying in line 36, "I think they want to please him too." Viktoria expressed her positive outlook in several lines in this episode, as she said in line 46 about one of her buddies, "his writing is really good." In line 57, she explained that "I'm kind of glad to have them," projecting a productive relationship with the two even further as she said in line 61, "I feel I can add more to that."

> 45. I kinda happy that I have them both/because they're both at like different sides

46. I have Ezekiel/he's like/his writing is really good and he was telling me things like

47. he likes to write because he can write his feelings down

48. and he said the hardest thing about being a writer is that he doesn't have enough time to write

49. and he needs to think about what to write

50. and I think it's like/I don't imagine a second grader saying that

51. and then you have George on the other side/who

52. he's like writing all over the place really big words and it's really sloppy

53. so it's like two different things

54. I couldn't even read George's name (V)

However, Viktoria used negative framing in line 50 when she posited, "I don't imagine a second grader saying [he needs to think about writing]" and further in line 52 when she evaluated her student writing in saying, "He's like writing all over the place, really big words and it's really sloppy" and in line 54 "I couldn't even read George's name."

5.3.2   March 20th

Later in the semester, Abigail used positive framing in line 67 when she says her student "wrote so much." Paulina framed her partner positively in lines 75–81 as she explained her writing strategies, later saying "she's really good at what she does" (line 86) and "she knew how to almost spell [inspired] too" (line 102). Abigail posited that the quantity of writing is a significant outcome in the classroom, positioning it as a strength of her student.

Viktoria invoked negative framing in this episode in line 106 when she said her student "can't change [his story] anymore" and in line 109 when she said, "he was just not having it today." In line 119, she explained, "he doesn't have a lot of details/he didn't want to add anything else." She projected in line 159 that "he's never going to have a story." Negative framing helps us understand, according to Fairclough, "what is the case and what is not the case in reality" (p. 125). Realities were constructed and reflected from figured worlds in that we recognize and assign significance to certain acts and outcomes. Viktoria's language reflected her belief and reality that George's attitude should be more cooperative and productive than what it was that day, and therefore negatively framed her student's writing behavior. This reality was constructed through Viktoria's figured world of teaching, where she believed with encouragement and support, he would change his mind and start to write.

5.3.3 Deictics

Wortham and Reyes (2015) explain that deictics can range from different aspects, like participants, information, and discursive topics. They list four types of deictics: spatial, temporal, person, and discourse. My PSTs mostly used discourse deictics. For example, in line 44, Viktoria said, "It's interesting," which stands in for future discourse as she clarifies later, "They're on different sides [of achievement]" (line 45). In line 125, Abigail told Viktoria, "Well I think my student is kind of like *that* too." This discourse deictic stood in for the prior discourse of the way Viktoria characterized her student as a reluctant writer. This demonstrates the ways a deictic could be employed by participants to further construe a social action; in this sense, the construction of a "reluctant writer" identity was further construed and configured.

5.4 Paulina and Viktoria: Discourse and Figured Worlds over Speech Events

Two PSTs' discourse emerged from the data in a way that I felt necessitates a final discussion. Paulina and Viktoria had completely different experiences this semester, which was reflected in their language. Paulina maintained positive framing in her language in both episodes and commented on the agency of her student often. From her figured world of teaching and learning, she valued certain outcomes from her work with her student, which is further realized by that student's work. Paulina's figured world of teaching and learning was reinscribed through her work with this particular student. However, Viktoria's frequent negative framing reflected her values of certain outcomes that are not realized by her partner. Viktoria's figured world of teaching and learning was contested, reflected in her negative framing and having to control student's agency. These figured worlds shaped how they positioned children in subsequent interactions in the writing classroom.

6 Implications

The findings of this analysis hold significant implications for teacher preparation and education. I discuss several considerations below.

6.1   Supporting Preservice Teachers' Emerging Professional Identity

The most significant implication of this analysis was to examine how we support preservice teachers' emerging professional identities. The ways we support our PSTs may determine their success in their subsequent classroom experiences. Disequilibrium is important for growth; indeed, Gelfuso and Dennis explain, "with equilibrium comes stasis (a slowing down or stopping)" (p. 80). The authors explain that equilibrium may occur when students' figured worlds are consistent with the ones they enter in the teaching field. Paulina's figured worlds gave her a sense of equilibrium, a sense of assurance that what she was doing worked, and she no longer needed to reach into her tool box or repertoire to support her student. Viktoria, on the other hand, in dealing with a challenging student, faced disequilibrium as she faced an inconsistency between the figured worlds of student, teaching, and learning. She expressed that she had tried everything to get her student to write. Preservice teachers will experience a range of encouraging and discouraging events in their training and most certainly in their professional life later. Whether it is equilibrium or disequilibrium that our PSTs face, it is our job to recognize the moments that we either support their professional decision-making, challenge their thinking (when appropriate; not when it can be cutting them down), provide new perspectives, and more so they can situate themselves within the figured worlds of teachers. We must recognize that PSTs arrive with their own set of knowledge, beliefs, and values and that they will affect the negotiation of future knowledge, beliefs, and values. This figured world includes new sets of activities, new actors and agents, and additional knowledges, beliefs, and values. We need to understand preservice educators and position them as those individuals that live in the "in-between," which produces its own set of knowledge, beliefs, and values. We cannot expect them to access the figured world of teaching and learning without some sort of internal conflict and without some sort of scaffolding and support.

6.2   Acknowledging Affect

Noteworthy is the evolution of student rewording through the use of synonyms to describe their second-grade partner. PSTs' language on February 6th contained much affective language, positioning children as objects of affective evaluation through words like "cute" and "sweet." However, their language contained little or no affective discourse, instead describing their children with achievement words like "smart," "good," and "gifted." We should expect our preservice teachers to position children as more than just objects of affection, as we hope our future teachers see their future students as competent and powerful, full of potential to transform our classrooms and the world that surrounds them. However, we still need to acknowledge that our teachers, especially elementary teachers, enter the profession because of the affection or fondness they have for working with children. It is that affection that preservice teachers can draw upon as they face trying times, like the challenges Viktoria faced with her partner. These are inevitable, but educators' love of children is something university faculty must continue to cultivate and acknowledge. Time spent with children, course readings, class discussions, field placements and more can help elevate preservice teachers' language about children and help them position children in ways outside of affect.

6.3   Overwording and Reported Speech

Preservice educators frequently relied on reported speech in their efforts to describe what took place with their students in each episode. Wortham and Reyes (2015) helped us understand that reported speech is a way our PSTs can take verbs of speaking to characterize participants in narrated and narrating events. These characterizations can lead to the construal and configuration of indexicals that lend itself to a particular social action. This analysis can help us understand when our PSTs use reported speech and what kind of characterizations they are using for their students. For it is their characterization of students that can lead to certain subject positions within their classroom, where students fall into certain categories based on what the teacher reports. Viktoria's reported speech above reflected a deficit view of her students instead of valuing the work he has already produced. In this sense, we use these moments of reported speech to potentially redirect PSTs' characterization of their students in hopes that they will characterize students on the assets they already have.

6.4   Discourse over Speech Events

One final implication of this discourse analysis is to examine PSTs over the course of speech events to understand the ways in which their utterances and cultural models travel over time as PSTs learn to be a teacher. We may only gather a shallow, isolated understanding of our PSTs and their knowledge, beliefs, and values if we analyze only one instance of their language-in-use.

Further research on preservice educators and their figured worlds would benefit university faculty in understanding how to support future teachers in clinical methods settings. We must also value our PSTs' prior figured worlds in helping them access the varied figured worlds of teaching and learning.

References

Burdelski, M., & Mitsuhashi, K. (2010). "She thinks you're Kawaii": Socializing affect, gender, and relationships in a Japanese preschool. *Language in Society, 39*(1), 65–93.

Fairclough, N. (1989). *Language and power.* New York, NY: Longman.

Gee, J. P. (1991). A linguistic approach to narrative. *Journal of Narrative and Life History, 1*(1), 15–39.

Gelfuso, A., & Dennis, D. V. (2017). Reproducing figured worlds of literacy teaching and learning: Examining the "language-in-use" of an inservice and preservice teacher enacting the practice of literacy planning. *Action in Teacher Education, 39*(1), 67–84.

Wortham, S., & Reyes, A. (2015). *Discourse analysis beyond the speech event.* New York, NY: Routledge.

Zeichner, K. (2010). Rethinking the connections between campus courses and field experiences in college-and university-based teacher education. *Journal of Teacher Education, 61*(1–2), 89–99.

Zeichner, K., & Bier, M. (2012). The turn toward practice and clinical experience in US teacher education. *Beiträge zur Lehrerbildung, 30*(2), 153–170.

Appendix A

Students' names have been abbreviated to their first initial (or first three letters of their name, since there are two students who have an "M" name) and have been left it at the end of their turn.

February 6th, Paulina, Michelle, Miranda, Abigail
I. Boys' friendship and writing as 'cute'
1. Um/well I had one little boy and he/talked and talked and talked and talked (Mic[1])
2. Oh really (A)
3. Yes he loved to talk/and he talked about like everything like
4. his motorcycles and all this stuff/and his best friend
5. and it was really cute
6. his best friend wrote his name on his heart map
7. and so then (Mic)
8. That's so cute (A)
9. Aw (Mir)
10. He found out that his best friend did it
11. and he was like/he wrote it on his heart map

POSITIONING STUDENTS AS WRITERS

12. because I think they're neighbors and they hang out like every day (Mic)
13. Oh that's so sweet (P)
14. and they just talked about what they did together it was so cute but
15. um he was a lot more focused on drawing than actually writing
16. so it was really hard to get him to like/want to write
17. cuz he wanted/to draw everything (Mic)

II. Girl on task as 'cute'
18. because I thought it was really cute
19. because um/she sat there and like
20. she my student/she talked to me
21. but everything was still focused on what it was supposed to be
22. we'd even get off/on a/completely different story talking about something
23. but she'd mention it and then she'd write it down
24. She was really cute (P)

III. Students' affection for teacher as 'cute'
25. I felt like the kids really respected Mr. Kurtzman and listened to him
26. because I saw a lot of kids writing "my teacher" on their heart maps (P)
27. Ohhhh! (Mir, Mic, A)
28. That's so cute (A)
29. That was really sweet (P)
30. So it sounds like you think if a child respects a teacher
31. it's partly because they are fond of the teacher? (E)
32. Right (Mir)
33. Mmhmm (A)
34. Yeah (Mo)
35. Yeah/definitely (P)

IV. Students' desire to please teachers as 'cute'
36. I think they want to please them too
37. like for our students right now
38. they were saying if you were given $100 what would you do?
39. and almost all of them said "I wanna buy Ms. Lewandowski a new outfit" (A)
40. Oh that's sweet (E)
41. Or I wanna give her some money
42. It was really cute
43. And she was like "Thank you!" (A)

February 6th, Louise, Bethany, and Viktoria
I. Viktoria projecting her excitement about two different students
44. But what I noticed is that/it's interesting
45. I kinda happy that I have them both/because they're both at like different sides
46. I have Ezekiel/he's like/his writing is really good and he was telling me things like
47. he likes to write because he can write his feelings down
48. and he said the hardest thing about being a writer is that he doesn't have enough time to write
49. and he needs to think about what to write
50. and I think it's like/I don't imagine a second grader saying that
51. and then you have George on the other side/who
52. he's like writing all over the place really big words and it's really sloppy
53. so it's like two different things
54. I couldn't even read George's name (V)
55. That's so cute (B)
56. But they're also in different places, which is really interesting (L)
57. That's why I'm kind of like/glad I have them
58. because I know I need to focus more on George/helping him with something
59. but also at the same time I can already improve on what Ezekiel has
60. cuz he's already up/he's really good
61. but I feel like I can add more to that? I don't know
62. I'm just excited they're both at like different levels (V)
63. I think if you had each/if you had them work together
64. cuz I'm sure there's something that one is good at/and the other's not
65. and they can use that together to build on their writing skills as a whole (L)

March 20th, Paulina, Michelle, Abigail, and Viktoria
I. Abigail's description of her partner's writing
66. He was [student]'s buddy/and he was really, really smart
67. like he wrote so much, but he just has a lot of trouble with spelling
68. I thought something that was really cute was
69. I was like asking them what the dog was
70. he was writing about a dog getting off the airplane/that was there for him
71. so I think he was talking about Miss Zuccaro's/her story
72. so I was asking him what he was looking like
73. and so he was writing like the dog had puppy eyes
74. I thought that was really cute (A)

POSITIONING STUDENTS AS WRITERS

II. Paulina reflects on the capabilities of her 'advanced' student
75. My student is like/insanely advanced in her writing
76. One of the things that I noticed that she did is
77. she's writing about/she's writing about her stuffed animal
78. and she's writing about their day at school together
79. and so she said "Mr. Kurtzman called *us* to the carpet"/but then she crossed off *us*
80. and she wrote *the class*/and I said "Well why did you do that?"
81. and she said "Well who's *us*?" (P)
82. Wow, she's smart
83. I don't even think/I would have caught that (A)
84. Really? Wow, that's really/that's good (Mic)
85. Like a lot of my 'next steps' for her/is really just to praise her on her efforts
86. because she's really good at what she does
87. I mean/she organized her paper/she had them laid out/
88. and then she put the paper/when we were finished working on it
89. she put it in order (P)
90. Wow
91. maybe she's part of the gifted and talented
92. I think they said like 5% of the students here/are gifted and talented (A)
93. Yeah/I mean/I've talked to Mr. Kurtzman ... about her before
94. and he said, "Yes she's like, extremely good" ...
95. she's the one/Miss Zuccaro asked/she said 'speak' (P)
96. Yeah I thought that was interesting
97. a second grader said speak (A)
98. Oh she's really good
99. I asked her/because she was using different verbs
100. and I asked her if she knew what *inspired* meant/and she knew that
101. so she's really really smart
102. And then she knew how to almost spell it too so (P)

III. Viktoria reflects on a challenging student
103. Well I'm having a really hard time with one of my students
104. Like/for the past few weeks/every week/he's changed his story (V)
105. Mmmm, that's really hard (A)
106. So I told him this time/he can't change it anymore/
107. two weeks ago/we talked about how we were going to combine what the stories were together
108. cuz they kind of relate/so I tried doing that
109. but he was just not having it today

110. he was like "I don't want to do it/I hate my life/don't ask me to do anything cuz I'm not/I hate writing"
111. so it was really hard for me to try to get him to like/do anything to it
112. and he just basically told me he wasn't going to change his story
113. he was just going to leave it as is (V)

IV. Viktoria describes her student's story
114. What's his story about? (A)
115. One of his stories is/about his grandma giving him rides
116. and another story was about his mom's car didn't work
117. and I was like "Oh put these together" but he said he doesn't want to
118. He just wants to talk about his mom getting the car fixed now
119. like he doesn't have a lot of details/he didn't want to add anything else
120. I tried asking him a lot of questions to get him to tell me like details/and he was just not having it
121. I even went through the thing and I basically wrote/"these are the parts of your story/how you can start it out"(V)
122. That's good (A)
123. And he was just trying to copy my sentences and I was like
124. "No this is not your story/this is your outline" (V)

V. Abigail offers advice from her experience
125. Well/I think my student is kind of like that too
126. and what helped him was/I liked asked him to write it on there
127. like just a couple words at a time
128. and then like draw his face next to it/and what it looked like
129. cuz he doesn't really like writing/he'd rather draw
130. so if your student's like that/you can just encourage more drawing
131. cuz at least they're telling the story(A)
132. I mean/I did tell him/do you want to add any drawings,/which he does have here
133. but he was like "I don't want to draw anymore"
134. So I was like you don't want to draw/you don't want to add words
135. I don't know what to do with you. (V)

VI. Paulina tries another approach for supporting Viktoria
136. Maybe you should try
137. Because one of the things I found is like
138. it's helpful but it's hard to get them to actually like write
139. it's just ask him to *tell* you the story

POSITIONING STUDENTS AS WRITERS

140. Be like "So what happened?"/and just let him talk about it
141. because maybe he doesn't want to like/he won't see it as work that way
142. Be like "Yeah but what happened?"/and then be like/"Oh, well do you want to include that in your story?" (P)

VII. Viktoria re-enacts a conversation with her student
143. Well I've tried that/like I have/"Tell me your story/what happened"
144. and he was like/"nothing/the car was broken"
145. and I was like/"How did it break?"
146. He's like "I don't know"
147. I was like "Something's wrong with it"/and he said "The engine"
148. and I was like/"Oh what happened to the engine?/How long was it broken?"
149. I tried asking him questions and/"What happened before that?/Who fixed the car?" (V)
150. Or maybe even encourage him/say
151. "Well do you want to write about something that you know a little more about?"
152. Like something happier/a fun story you WANT to talk about?"
153. Maybe find out his interests and then be like
154. "Oh well, do you want to write a story about that?" (P)
155. But I mean/I feel like at this point/if I do that
156. like I'm not going to have time to do all of it
157. because he's written about the broken engine/his grandma giving him rides/him eating pizza
158. and I'm like at this point/if he keeps changing the story
159. he's never going to have the story (V)
160. But maybe he doesn't really need to
161. if he can't get to that level ... (A)

BRIDGING THE THEME

Inquiry Matters

Mikkaka Overstreet and Lori Norton-Meier

The act of inquiry is central to our work. Asking questions about our practice, investigating those questions, and using that data collection and analysis to inform our reflective action in the classroom is critical to our work as teacher educators and scholars. However, we also create spaces for our preservice teachers (PSTs) to engage in the act of inquiry. Our expectation is not to simply consume knowledge but to engage our PSTs in the act of purposefully asking questions about children's learning and the opportunities we make available as teachers. In the previous chapter, Emily Zuccaro explores the discourse practices of her PSTs and creates a space for them to engage in a deep analysis of literacy practices and dialogic pedagogy. Also, Anetria Swanson presents the story of a first-year teacher that details his ongoing inquiry about the act of teaching and learning. The first-year teacher and Swanson dig deeply and theoretically to unpack the layers of transitioning from a teacher education program to his first teaching job that helps all of us understand the messy reality of learning to be a teacher in urban partnerships.

CHAPTER 9

Perspectives from a First-Year Teacher

Anetria Swanson

Abstract

This chapter will shed insight into experiences that shape a beginning teacher's professional identity during the transition from their preservice to in-service year. Urrieta (2007) writes " Identity is ... very much about how people come to understand themselves, how they come to *figure* out who they are, through the *worlds* that they participate in and how they relate to others within and outside of these worlds." With a focus on identity and figured worlds, this research uncovers how experiences during the preservice and in-service years shape the identity of beginning teachers and contribute to their figured worlds. Using an interpretivist approach, a first-year teacher was interviewed using narrative inquiry as the methodology. Glesne (2016) asserts reality is socially constructed, complex, and ever changing and there is emphasis on uncovering how people interpret and make meaning of their lived experiences.

Pillen, Beijaard, and Brok (2013) believe new teachers experience professional identity tensions in which there is conflict between their own personal knowledge, beliefs, attitudes, norms, and values, and that of their new school environment. Beginning teachers are often torn between what they know and believe to be best practice based on preservice teachings and practicum experiences, and the reality they experience in their in-service placements. This narrative study will uncover the tensions Pillen et al. (2013) outline, including experiencing conflicts between one's own and other's orientations regarding learning to teach, being exposed to contradictory institutional attitudes, and feeling incompetent in terms of knowledge (e.g., content and classroom management). Additionally, this work seeks to consider the implications of not addressing known tensions and ways to develop support structures that counter the tensions.

Keywords

figured worlds – identity – new teachers

1 Introduction

As an African-American female raised in a city known as the "Gateway to the South," I have developed my cultural identity over time through interactions across multiple contexts—familial, educational, and occupational. Identity is not static. It is a result of the interactions between lived experiences and figured worlds. According to Gee, a figured world is "a theory, story, model, or image of a simplified world that captures what is taken to be typical or normal about people, practices, things, or interactions" (Gee, 2014). Urrieta (2007) agrees with Gee when she writes, "Identity is also very much about how people come to understand themselves, how they come to *figure* out who they are, through the *worlds* that they participate in and how they relate to others within and outside of these worlds" (emphasis added).

My maternal grandmother left the Jim Crow south, specifically Tuscaloosa, Alabama, in search of better jobs and opportunities in Louisville. Even though she found the racial climate to be better than that of her hometown in Alabama, she continued to struggle with the remnants of racism as she built a new life for her family in Louisville. It is in the church that she found refuge from the harsh realities of being an African-American and single mother to five children. The church and what it meant to her—specifically the extended family and sense of community—is what strengthened and sustained her. It is through her example that I understand how her life was shaped across contexts of time, place, and space. I can also understand how my grandmother's lived experiences shaped her identity as a mother, grandmother, and member of a faith-based community during a tumultuous time in our country's history. Her figured worlds shifted from the harsh realities of discrimination and segregation in rural Alabama to less overt discrimination in "the Gateway to the South."

In examining my identity through an *educational* context, I can see how my experiences in grades K-12 and even today have shaped me as a learner as described by Malone and Barabino (2008). I often was "the only one" (i.e., African-American student) in my classes. At an early age, I was placed in Advanced Program classes. These classes tended to have few or no students that looked like me, pushing me into the insider/outsider status. I felt alone within my classes where I was "the only one" as well as isolated from fellow African-American students who were in the other classes. Additionally, throughout my whole K-12 experience, I had a total of three African-American teachers—none in high school. Looking back on these years, I realize my positionality impacted my identity as a student, learner, and future educator.

Similarly, within the *occupational* context, I often found myself in situations where I was the "only one," delicately balancing my interactions and professional relationships while maintaining my own way of thinking, believing, and valuing. In workspaces, more so than any other, I am mindful of how discourses are constantly being used to enact relationships, identities, and even connections. As an African-American female in the workplace, I am mindful of stereotypes such as the "angry black female" and the potential for individuals to project identities onto others (Overstreet, 2019).

Just as my identity has changed over time based on my lived experiences in a variety of contexts, the identity of a teacher changes from preservice to in-service relative to their lived experiences and figured worlds.

2 Literature Review

I have recently immersed myself in research focused on trends and issues in teacher recruitment and retention, a growing interest that has developed through my role in the Human Resources department of one of the largest school districts in my state. Recent research focused on preservice and beginning teachers suggests that many teachers struggle to cultivate classroom environments that facilitate student learning and that novice teachers have low self-efficacy as it relates to their beliefs about their preparedness to work with diverse populations (Siwatu, 2011a). As a Human Resources professional with a background in teaching, curriculum and instruction, and instructional coaching, my unique position has allowed me to support new hires through three key junctures in their careers: preservice (student teaching and/or practicum placements), post preservice (recruitment and hiring), and onboarding (e.g. new teacher induction and internship). This lens has led me to ponder several questions related to new teacher identity: What are new teachers' figured worlds? What factors promote or limit new teacher retention in the context of a new teacher's figured world?

Siwatu (2011b) argues that teacher self-efficacy is a critical variable in teacher retention. Teachers whose self-efficacy beliefs indicate that they are ill-prepared to teach in culturally and linguistically diverse settings combined with having inadequate experiences in their teacher preparation program are at risk for leaving the profession prematurely. Siwatu's theory of teacher self-efficacy is extremely useful because it sheds insight on the challenges faced by teachers during their first year, especially as it relates to tensions they encounter while developing their professional identity as a teacher. Pillen, Beijaard,

and Brok (2013) believe new teachers experience professional identity tensions in which there is conflict between their own personal knowledge, beliefs, attitudes, norms, and values and that of their new school environment. My experience in working with beginning teachers during their internship year confirms that beginning teachers are often torn between what they know and believe to be best practice and what is expected of them by the school administration. In working with first-year teachers, I have observed the tensions Pillen et al. (2013) outline, including:
- experiencing conflicts between one's own and other's orientations regarding learning to teach,
- being exposed to contradictory institutional attitudes, and
- feeling incompetent in terms of knowledge (e.g., content and classroom management).

My curiosity about identity and figured worlds led me to a conversation with a first-year teacher. I hoped to uncover how lived experiences during the first year contributed to the teacher's figured worlds, shaped the identity of a first-year teacher, and promoted or limited retention. It is my belief that these tensions experienced during the critical first year influence developing teacher identities and impact teacher retention.

3   Methods

During the spring of 2015, I interviewed a first-year teacher, identified as XM, during the eighth month of his tenure at Smith Elementary School. The district's teacher retention rate during the 2014–2015 school year was 88.4% while the school's teacher retention rate was significantly lower at 79.4%. The 2014–2015 school year presented significant staffing challenges, with a 20.6 % decline in retention from the previous year. Table 9.1 reveals stable teacher retention across the district from 2009–2016. When compared to district retention rates, XM's school's teacher retention rate had significant drops during the 2012–2013 and 2014–2015 school years. During the 2012–2013 school year there was a drop in retention, which rebounded during the 2013–2014 school year. During the 2014–2015 school year, there was another drop in retention from 100.0% the previous school year, to 79.4%.

Smith Elementary, located in the southeast part of an urban school district in Kentucky, had a school enrollment consisting of approximately 375 students with the following demographics: 46.8% White, 28.2% African-American, 17.8% Hispanic, and 7.2% other, and 9.6% English as Second Language (ESL). Approximately 76% of the students qualified for the Free/Reduced Lunch

TABLE 9.1   School and district teacher retention data (provided by school district)

	% retention 2009–2010	% retention 2010–2011	% retention 2011–2012	% retention 2012–2013	% retention 2013–2014	% retention 2014–2015	% retention 2015–2016
School	92.0	92.9	100.0	83.3	100.0	79.4	96.0
District	90.0	88.4	95.8	89.7	90.5	88.4	87.2

program. The school was led by a first-year principal, who had recently been appointed.

Before the interview, I decided to utilize a semi-structured questioning process to elicit responses related to successes and challenges (tensions) experienced during the first year. Merriam (2009) characterizes semi-structured interviews as having flexibly worded questions, including a mixture of structured and non-structured questions. Merriam notes, "Neither the exact wording nor the order of questions is determined ahead of time" (Merriam, 2009, p. 90). The semi-structured format allowed me the freedom to change the order of questions and probe when necessary to better capture my interviewee's feelings. During the transcription process, I was looking for insight into XMs self-efficacy beliefs and how discourses were shaping his identity(ies) as a new teacher. Additionally, I hoped to uncover if there were any shifts in XMs positionality as a new teacher and if so, when did those shifts occur (e.g., from preservice to in-service) and why?. I leaned on Gee's description of an ideal discourse analysis using his building tasks and tools of inquiry to uncover XM's figured worlds and how they shaped his identity as a new teacher (Gee, 2014). Using Gee's building tasks and tools of inquiry, questions I explored included:

- How do experiences during the first-year contribute to XM's figured world(s) and shape his identity as a first-year teacher?
- How are discourses being used to create, distribute, or withhold social goods?
- How are figured worlds being used to build and sustain relationships with students and other staff members?

Throughout the interview, I categorized the responses of XM into two categories: (a) experiences associated with promoting teacher retention and (b) experiences associated with limiting teacher retention. After I categorized XM's responses, I coded and organized them into themes. By utilizing Gee's building tasks (identity) and tools of inquiry (figured world), in question #1,

I noticed XM's responses indicate frustration he felt when working with his team leader. XM's figured world reveals the belief that teachers at Smith Elementary do not plan together or support each other. I believe this figured world is rooted in experiences associated with limiting teacher retention. In the second question, which delves into the relationship between discourse and politics, I again observed XM's frustration, this time with not having access to needed resources. I coded this experience like the one presented in question #1, as an experience associated with limiting teacher retention. Lastly, in question #3, which examined how figured worlds were being used to build and sustain relationships, I observed a lack of positive professional relationships in which XM could engage. This was coded as another experience associated with limiting teacher retention.

4 Findings

My use of Gee's building tasks and tools of inquiry provided insight into XM's beliefs about his experiences as a first-year teacher. I was able to code XM's responses to the interview questions based on the likelihood of promoting or limiting teacher retention. One theme I recognized in lines 4–15 was motivation for entering the teaching profession. In this section, when asked what his hopes, dreams, and aspirations were upon entering the profession, XM discusses the belief that he can make a difference in the lives of his students. For example, XM recalls:

> Well, I had had a really positive experience with teachers my whole life, umm coming from kind of a fractured family background where my father got divorced three times and changing families and things like that and moving geographically and during all that time umm especially in elementary school, the teachers had been a consistent resource in my life and so that was part of the wanting to become a teacher and also, so for me having relationships with the kids just seemed like it was a big motivation and you know it's kind of cliché but making a difference in the life of children in a world that is kind of messed up and I think it is kind of idealistic to want to teach kids and you know it is cliché again but I like the idea of teaching kids so that maybe you know the world can be a different place than the world they are born into.

He discusses this theme again in lines 115–118, when he mentioned his belief that he is making a difference in the lives of his students as he helps them to make sense of the world around them.

Another theme I observed was interactive classroom discourse. When asking XM to share moments that have brought him happiness in the classroom, he mentions class discussions, students making contributions, discussing current events, and relating to students' experiences as being positive in lines 109–113. This helped me to uncover his figured world as it related to student engagement and creating meaningful learning opportunities for students.

I agree with Urrieta (2007) that figured worlds are "socially produced, culturally constituted activities." It is in these worlds where people come to conceptually and procedurally produce new self-understandings. These new understandings are undoubtedly linked to shifts in XM's self-efficacy beliefs and identity as a developing first-year teacher.

XM's responses also offered insight into how his experiences could limit teacher retention. One theme I uncovered was lack of collegiality. XM discusses frustration with the Professional Learning Community (PLC) process in his in-service setting in lines 35–38. He reflects:

> ... I didn't understand why at the school that I was assigned to ... there wasn't PLC planning and I thought it was a district-wide mandate whereas at my student teaching school and every other school I've been to was fairly strong ...

Pillen et al. (2013) would argue this occurrence is a tension—being exposed to contradictory institutional attitudes. XM mentions the contradictory approaches to PLCs in his preservice and in-service school experiences. In lines 64–66, XM again reflects on his negative start to the school year as it relates to support from team teachers and common planning. This discussion presented another theme related to the same tension—inconsistency across schools—as XM notes the difference between his current school and the school where he completed his student teaching.

Another prevalent theme related to limiting teacher retention was hardship in setting up the classroom and access to supplies. In lines 29–33, XM shares his early frustrations of getting his room set up and not understanding the district's curricular programs and how they were supposed to be implemented in the context of his fourth-grade classroom. García, Arias, Harris Murri, and Serna (2010) share three general areas of knowledge they believe teachers should acquire: knowledge of learners and how they learn and develop within social context, conceptions of curriculum and social purposes of education, and lastly, an understanding of teaching. XM seems to indicate a lack of knowledge in these three areas as evidenced by his frustration with not understanding district curriculum resources and also not knowing how to develop a lesson. In lines 272–278, XM discusses this tension by saying:

> So when I was writing lessons having subbed for a year and a half, and I hadn't written lessons in a year ... I was thinking so ... how do I communicate this information with these kids. And looking at the structure I mean I knew ... intellectually ... yeah ... I need an objective and then I am going to have activities that tie to it and I am going to try and assess that etc., but it in terms of you know ... how does it work? How do you create from nothing all of these ideas and all of this information you have and all of this stuff you have as a student teacher and stuff I had gathered?

By October of his first year of teaching, XM had lost so much confidence in his ability to plan lessons that he wrote me the following email message:

> I was wondering if you know any retired 4th grade teachers who might like to make thirty dollars an hour to help me plan on Saturdays. I really want to be successful this year. ... It may sound silly to pay someone, but it would be worth it for me to get better support.

XM's frustrations with the lack of collegial support were evident in the following email message, also sent in October:

> The basic problem is that my team leader doesn't believe in planning together, so I literally don't get to even see his planning book. So I spend 20 hours each weekend planning alone, and though I'm writing plans I have so little experience they're just not that good. ... I follow the books but it's like here's a book, go teach from it with no guidance. ... I don't know, maybe I picked the wrong career. I just wonder what it would be like to be at a school where I was really planning again, I would have had such a better year.

Additionally, in lines 66–74, XM comments on how other teachers would not share resources such as a pencil sharpener, illuminating the fact of how hard it was to get support initially from colleagues and access to basic classroom supplies. He notes:

> I mean literally other teachers would not let me use their pencil sharpener. They would say, 'Oh, you can use it but it is really it's kind of broken. It doesn't work that well.' And I understand now why they said that. I don't know that I would want a new teacher using mine everyday either. But then I would walk by their rooms and hear them sharpening all of their pencils and it was just hard to get support and even supplies at some stage of the game but umm but those things are just beginning things and

so I would say part of my being happy about the situation now is umm reflecting on the way it was in the beginning.

Although I agree that the tensions presented by Pillen et al. (2013) contribute to limiting teacher retention, I also recognize the list is not exhaustive. Additional tensions are revealed through XM's interview, such as lack of collegiality and inconsistency among resources.

In lines 120–126, XM recalls with sarcasm the moment when he finally received a pencil sharpener, several months into the school year. XM's longing for collegiality and the team dynamics he grew accustomed to during his preservice experience underscores the notion that social goods are relevant and at stake in the context of a first-year teacher and raises the issue of how social goods are being distributed. Earlier, I called upon Gee's building task of politics to determine how discourses are being used by XM to create, distribute, or withhold social goods. Gee (2014) defines politics as using language to give or take away social goods or to project how social goods ought to be distributed. In lines 407–422, XM wrestles with the idea of how he will negotiate for the resources (social goods) he needs, by saying:

> Just an overview, looking around the room, somebody that is more experienced who would maybe be an advocate for you so that for example ... I just casually mentioned to my principal that I didn't have a table and that it was hard to get one ... I did eventually negotiate with another teacher for a table that he had ... that he didn't use his table ... but where my original one went, nobody knew. If you didn't have to negotiate for things you could go to someone and say " I need this. This is supposed to be in my room. Can you help me get it?" That would be helpful. Because every room should have certain things ... You shouldn't have to ... when you are new ... for example ... when you are a student teacher and you are collaborating ... you don't know how to do that. So when you are doing your first year ... how do you advocate for yourself that hey ... you have two computer tables .... I have none. You are a senior teacher who might yell at my kids in the hallway ... you know ... in terms of personality or practice. And you know ... so how do I now as an ex sub now come in as a new teacher and get out of your room what I need or you know ... and that kind of leads to some other things to in terms of relationships with other teachers.

Throughout the interview, XM revealed ways his attitudes and feelings about the teaching profession as well as his self-efficacy beliefs had shifted. Perhaps the introduction of a new principal (lines 49–53) and a revived sense of expectations with collaborative team processes such as PLCs and team planning presented a turning point in XM's experiences, as he discusses a positive shift in his overall attitude about the teaching profession (lines 21–25).

Additionally, when asked what he wishes he had known before the start of his first year, in lines 535–549, XM discusses how he believes he has "turned a corner" with his kids, based on getting to know his students and how to handle them. He declares:

> I wish I would have known that at some point magically something would click right around the winter break where I decide to run my class a certain way but also I knew the kids well enough to run it a certain way. I don't know if it's the word confidence but you kind of slow down. For example, I know them really well and I have seen them at their worst and I've seen them at their worst when I didn't know how to handle them at their worst and now I know how to handle them at their worst. It's not a really a day where something is going to happen where I am not going to know what to do. So that allows me to have the freedom to joke with them sometimes and keep it … even if it is a serious thing that I am dealing with … to keep it light in a way that I know that I can maintain control of the room and get it back to where it needs to go and I get through the day and successfully you know … get my stuff done and having passed Cycle II you know … I know that I am going to be a teacher next year and probably in the same school and that I can do the job and that I know these kids. So that piece of it … I wish I had known that at some point, I would turn a corner with them where our relationship would change based on me knowing what I didn't know before.

5 Discussion and Final Thoughts

Urrieta (2007) notes, "People figure out who they are through the activities and in relation to the social types that populate these figured worlds and in social relationships with the people who perform these worlds. People develop new identities in figured worlds." The essence of Urietta's argument is that figured worlds cultivate identities. Teacher identity is not static, but rather shaped by lived experiences. New teachers, like XM, have the potential to develop new identities in the context of varied figured worlds. XM's responses indicate a shift in his professional identity that has taken shape as a result of the following:
– building relationships with students,
– increased administrative support,

- opportunities for meaningful classroom interactions, and
- access to needed instructional resources.

It is my belief that these positive experiences have the potential to counter the tensions experienced early in the school year by XM and promote the likelihood of retention. These findings are significant because they provide insight into the professional development needs of first-year teachers as well as into establishing district and school policies to support new teachers.

McCann (2005) presents strategies that schools can employ to better support new teachers like XM. Suggestions include planning for mentoring, professional development centered on working with curriculum materials, connecting new staff members with key contacts (e.g., veteran staff members, in-school resources staff, and district-level staff supports), monitoring new teacher experiences through observation and ongoing dialogue, and being proactive in supporting new teachers through known challenges/experiences typical of the first year. These strategies can provide schools insight into ways to address those experiences likely to limit teacher retention, while building upon support structures known to promote teacher retention.

Additionally, XM's responses indicated a need for additional experiences within the context of his preservice work. Experiencing a figured world centered on collaboration and teachers working consistently in professional learning communities during his preservice years may have been a double-edged sword. Undoubtedly, being exposed to effective collaborative structures positively impacted XM's professional identity. However, when immersed in a professional culture with little or no professional interactions among grade level staff, XM lost his belief in his ability to plan lessons and cultivate classroom culture. This signals the importance of varied experiences at the preservice level which thrusts preservice teachers into what psychologist Lev Vygotsky calls the "zone of proximal development." The zone of proximal development reflects the difference between what one can do without help and with help. Under current state guidelines, preservice teachers complete their student teacher semester under the mentorship of a cooperating teacher. During a semester-long placement, the preservice teacher works alongside the mentor teacher, utilizing one or more collaborative co-teaching strategies from St. Cloud University, Teacher Quality Enhancement Center (2011). See Table 9.2 for an overview of the co-teaching strategies.

After spending a semester immersed in a collaborative structure centered on seven co-teaching strategies, in addition to being in a professional development model school, XM's identity as a teacher was being shaped. When hired to teach in a setting that was the polar opposite, his identity shifted, based on the social practices of his in-service setting. He had low self-efficacy and a

TABLE 9.2 Seven co-teaching strategies

Strategy	Definition/Example
One Teach, One Observe	One teacher has primary responsibility while the other gathers specific observational information on students or the (instructing) teacher. The key to this strategy is to focus the observation – where the teacher doing the observation is observing specific behaviors.
One Teach, One Assist	An extension of One Teach, One Observe. One teacher has primary instructional responsibility while the other assists students with their work, monitors behaviors, or corrects assignments.
Station Teaching	The co-teaching pair divides the instructional content into parts – Each teacher instructs one of the groups, groups then rotate or spend a designated amount of time at each station – often an independent station will be used along with the teacher led stations.
Parallel Teaching	Each teacher instructs half the students. The two teachers are addressing the same instructional material and presenting the material using the same teaching strategy. The greatest benefit to this approach is the reduction of student to teacher ratio.
Supplemental Teaching	This strategy allows one teacher to work with students at their expected grade level, while the other teacher works with those students who need the information and/or materials retaught, extended or remediated.
Alternative (Differentiated)	Alternative teaching strategies provide two different approaches to teaching the same information. The learning outcome is the same for all students however the avenue for getting there is different.
Team Teaching	Well planned, team taught lessons, exhibit an invisible flow of instruction with no prescribed division of authority. Using a team teaching strategy, both teachers are actively involved in the lesson. From a students' perspective, there is no clearly defined leader – as both teachers share the instruction, are free to interject information, and available to assist students and answer questions

loss of confidence in himself as a teacher. Teacher education programs should takes steps to assure that student teachers can demonstrate independence when support is not present and have the ability to transfer their knowledge and experiences from preservice to in-service settings.

Currently, the focus on one teacher, XM, presents a limitation to my findings. After interviewing XM, I was left wondering what I would discover through further comparison among first-year teachers in similar environments, including ways new teachers are finding success or frustration during their first year. There is a need to expand this study to include additional first-year teachers in similar settings. Additionally, I believe there is much to learn about the first-year teacher's experience through using Gee's building tasks and tools of inquiry to further explore Pillen et al.'s tensions. For example, I hope to build upon my understanding of Gee's building tasks and tools of inquiry to uncover how first-year teachers utilize social language to enact or depict identities (teacher and student) in the classroom as well as tap into other building tasks and tools in inquiry. However, questions such as these can't be answered based solely on one interview alone.

More research is needed, focused on first-year teachers across multiple settings and also classroom data in terms of interactions between first-year teachers, their colleagues, supervisors, and students. It is worth mentioning that three new teachers were interviewed. I selected to focus on XM because his narrative stood out as having clear cut implications for teacher education professionals preparing preservice teachers to transition into in-service roles. Additionally, I found him interesting because, early in the school year, he had such low self-efficacy and was having an experience clearly headed toward his leaving the profession by the end of the year. Yet, in March, he emailed me, "I am really proud because I'm a real teacher now." XM's identity of himself as a real teacher continues. He will begin his fourth year of teaching this fall.

References

García, E., Arias, M. B., Harris Murri, N. J., & Serna, C. (2010). Developing responsive teachers: A challenge for a demographic reality. *Journal of Teacher Education, 61*(1–2), 132–142. doi:10.1177/0022487109347878

Gee, J. P. (2014). *An introduction to discourse analysis theory and method.* New York, NY: Routledge.

Malone, K. R., & Barabino, G. (2009). Narrations of race in STEM research settings: Identity formation and its discontents. *Science Education, 93*(3), 485–510. https://doi.org/10.1002/sce.20307

McCann, T. M., Johannessen, L. R., & Ricca, B. P. (2005). *Supporting beginning English teachers: Research and implications for teacher induction.* Urbana, IL: National Council for Teachers of English.

Merriam, S. B. (2009). *Qualitative research: A guide to design and implementation.* San Francisco, CA: Jossey-Bass.

Overstreet, M. (2019). My first year in academia or the mythical Black woman superhero takes on the Ivory Tower. *Journal of Women and Gender in Higher Education, 12*(1), 18–34.

Pillen, M., Beijaard, D., & den Brok, P. (2013). Tensions in beginning teachers' professional identity development, accompanying feelings and coping strategies. *European Journal of Teacher Education, 36*(3), 240–260. doi:10.1080/02619768.2012.696192

Siwatu, K. O. (2011a). Preservice teachers' culturally responsive teaching self-efficacy-forming experiences: A mixed methods study. *Journal of Educational Research, 104*(5), 360–369. doi:10.1080/00220671.2010.487081

Siwatu, K. O. (2011b). Preservice teachers' sense of preparedness and self-efficacy to teach in America's urban and suburban schools: Does context matter? *Teaching and Teacher Education, 27*(2), 357–365.

Urrieta, L. (2007). Figured worlds and education: An introduction to the special issue, editorial. *Urban Review, 39*(2), 107–116. Retrieved from http://search.ebscohost.com/login.aspx?direct=true&db=a9h&AN=25353569&site=ehost-live

BRIDGING THE THEME

Argument Matters

Mikkaka Overstreet and Lori Norton-Meier

As the title of this book indicates, this is complex work. It is difficult and messy and ongoing. It is not the sort of thing about which we can afford to get complacent. All parties involved must keep reflecting, keep troubling our thinking, keep pushing and questioning. We have to work at it and we have to argue for it. The heart of argument is negotiation. Negotiating new information. Challenging old understandings. Asking questions, gathering data, arguing from evidence, making claims from that evidence, and negotiating with others while reflecting on what we know differently now after the opportunity to inquire about teaching and learning. A foundation of argument reminds us to be critical and to look beyond simple answers to the complex problems of pedagogy in practice.

In the previous chapter, Anetria Swanson challenged us to think about how partnerships matter when teachers move from a preservice program into the field. She asked tough questions about the effectiveness of teacher education programs and about how districts and schools support first-year teachers. In the final chapter, Lori Norton-Meier and Mikkaka Overstreet draw this text to a conclusion by summarizing key ideas and argue for a new model in the preparation of teachers in urban, clinical settings.

CHAPTER 10

Conclusion: Lessons Learned from Research and Practice on the Path to "Ideological Becoming"

Lori Norton-Meier and Mikkaka Overstreet

Abstract

No one book can tell the entire story. Real, human stories do not have succinct beginnings, middles, and ends. This work is ongoing. This story is ongoing. There are many characters we haven't heard from here and many settings we have yet to explore. So, while this conclusion wraps up this particular anthology, it is more of a "to be continued" than "the end".

Though there are implications here for a great deal more research to be done, these stories matter. If the field of education is to understand the potential, benefits, and necessities of clinical partnerships, then we need to share and examine the nature of partnership work across the country. As we noted in the introduction, despite the agreement on the necessity of clinical practice and the call for more consistency in its enactment, educational leaders agree that these partnerships must vary in consideration of local contexts (AACTE, 2018). In layman's terms "it's the context, stupid: general "best practices" have limited possibilities for addressing local contingencies in learning to teach" (Smagorinsky, 2018, p. 282). We need to see the characters (school and university partnership members) in a variety of settings.

In the Conclusion, we build a model that emerges from the previous chapters and pushes us to consider the way we structure and design opportunities for preservice and inservice teacher learning.

Keywords

teacher preparation – identity – ideological becoming – Bakhtin – clinical partnerships

CONCLUSION

1   Introduction

> I can honestly say that the most important part of my experience here is what happened in Ms. Morgan's 4th grade classroom. It was there that Marisol, Ahmad, and others challenged me to see the world through their eyes and my relationship with each and every one of them has taught me more than any reading, any project, any task. Probably the most important part? Every day I stare in the face of the *messy reality of this work* we call teaching. It is emotional. It takes every thought I have about skills, strategies, and expectations but every day I am thankful that I am here. (Danielle, a junior in teacher education; emphasis added)

This book is about Danielle and the preservice teachers like her who explore the messy realities of becoming a teacher in urban elementary classrooms. No one book can tell the entire story. Real, human stories do not have succinct beginnings, middles, and ends. This work is ongoing. This story is ongoing. There are many characters we haven't heard from here and many settings we have yet to explore. So, while this conclusion wraps up this particular anthology, it is more of a "to be continued" than a "the end."

Though there are implications here for a great deal more research to be done, these stories matter. If the field of education is to understand the potential, benefits, and necessities of clinical partnerships, then we need to share and examine the nature of partnership work across the country. As we noted in the introduction, despite the agreement on the necessity of clinical practice and the call for more consistency in its enactment, educational leaders agree that these partnerships must vary in consideration of local contexts (AACTE, 2018). In layman's terms "it's the context, stupid: general "best practices" have limited possibilities for addressing local contingencies in learning to teach" (Smagorinsky, 2018, p. 282). We need to see the characters (school and university partnership members) in a variety of settings. Throughout the case stories presented by the chapter authors in this text, we have worked to connect the stories by a text feature called, "Bridging the Theme." In this final chapter, we will offer a new perspective on the clinical preparation of teachers revealing what emerged as elements that *"matter"* and how these elements can come together in a new model for consideration as well as implications and setting the stage for the continuing work to inform our ongoing inquiries into the pathways of preparing future teachers.

2 The Act and Process of Ideological Becoming: A Model for Consideration

Throughout the chapter case stories in this text, each author tells his or her unique path to "ideological becoming." The thinking that fuels the term "ideological becoming" emerges from the work of Bakhtin who wrote about the "ideological self," reflecting his thinking that "human consciousness does not come into contact with existence directly, but through the medium of the surrounding ideological world" (Bakhtin & Medvedev, 1928/1978, p. 14). In essence, ideological becoming is "the process of selectively assimilating the words of others" (Bakhtin, 1981, p. 341) and indicating a set of community-shared viewpoints. Thus, all learning is a social act, oftentimes rooted in the hybridity of cultural identities. (Love, 2015, pp. 115–116).

Yet, this question persists. What is it that we as teachers of teachers can create, opportunities that can be orchestrated, dialogue that can be engaged, activities and moments of learning that can emerge that open up the possibility for each preservice teacher to continue on their own journey of ideological becoming? Throughout the case stories presented in this text and the "bridging the theme" connections, we revealed that six things matter: Identity, Relationships, Stories, Reflective Action, Inquiry as Stance, and Argument. A model of how we conceptualize these elements of ideological becoming are represented graphically in Figure 10.1. We purposefully nest these six elements with identity at the center, at the very core and the basis for all the other elements noting that without firmly embedding our courses and programs starting with an individual's intersecting identities, the other elements will struggle to exist and support each preservice teacher in ideological becoming. In the following paragraphs, we will re-visit each element and how we see it fitting into the messy reality of teacher preparation in clinical partnerships.

2.1   *Identity*

Throughout each of the chapters in this text, an uncovering of preservice teachers' exploration of their identities as well as their developing identity as teacher is at the very core of the work we do in teacher preparation. Moje and Luke (2009) describe "identity as something fluid and dynamic that is produced, generated, developed, or narrated over time" (p. 416). In Chapter 6, Tammi Davis described a documentary account of preservice teachers who moved from viewing themselves as "saviors" educating disadvantaged youths to seeing themselves as "safety nets" in place to support students as needed, the shift in their perceptions of their own identities helped them to reject deficit perspectives of the children in the partnership school. Then in Chapter 7

CONCLUSION 133

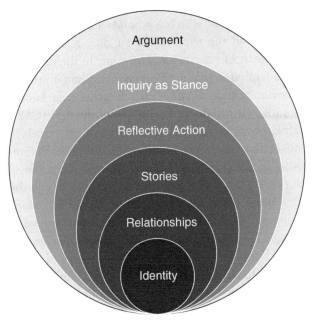

FIGURE 10.1   Bridging a new model of "ideological becoming" in clinical teacher preparation

and using intersectionality as a lens, Bianca Nightengale-Lee complicates PSTs understanding of themselves and others illuminating this notion of identity not as singular but the emerging understanding of individual's multiple intersecting identities. Her work challenges us to complicate our approaches to thinking and teaching about diversity in school settings where each PST's understanding of self and other confronts the "messy reality" of both personal and social lenses on teaching and learning. In each of these examples, exploration and growth is spurred by meaningful field experiences. CAEP Standard 2 requires that "effective partnerships and high-quality clinical practice are central to preparation so that candidates develop the knowledge, skills, and *professional dispositions* necessary to demonstrate positive impact on all P-12 students' learning and development" (CAEP, 2019, emphasis added). The research featured in this anthology suggests that the identity work necessary to truly internalizing the professional dispositions that value, affirm, and positively impact *all* students can only be achieved when quality teacher education coursework is paired with significant field experiences.

2.2   *Relationships*

Once we begin to explore the complexities of our developing identities, the relationships we build with practicing teachers, parents and families, and of course elementary age children become impactful opportunities on the journey to ideological becoming. Anyone who has ever taken a course in education has heard extensively about the necessity of building relationships. Relationships are at the very heart of teaching and learning. In the rationale for CAEP Standard 2, we are reminded that field experiences should provide preservice teachers an opportunity to be a part of an 'interactive professional community' with opportunities for collaboration and peer feedback" (CAEP, 2019). Thus, clinical partnerships are founded on reciprocal relationships between universities, schools, and communities. The nature of these relationships determines the nature of the partnerships. Will there be surface-level engagement (worth great press, but not necessarily great impact), or will the parties involved manage the heavy work of building trust and a shared vision? In Chapter 4, Lateefah Id-Deen and her co-authors helped us to envision what relationships should and could look like in university-school partnerships followed by Chapter 5 where Mikkaka Overstreet describes the process and messy reality of building such relationships. It is from this relationship-building that our students begin their own narratives of teaching and learning—stories of children and the layers of meaning around their future students that contribute to their sensemaking about becoming a teacher.

2.3 *Stories*

In the Introduction to this text, we explored the importance of stories. In each case story, the authors have illustrated the ability of stories to both clarify and complicate our understandings. As explained in CAEP Standard 2, field experiences should be of "sufficient depth, breadth, diversity, coherence, and duration to ensure that candidates demonstrate their developing effectiveness and positive impact on all students' learning and development" (CAEP, 2019). Preservice teachers need more than a single story if they are to develop a complete and asset-based view of all children (Tschida, Ryan, & Ticknor, 2014) and, consequently, the skills and dispositions to effectively teach them. Stories are unique to their contexts, but collectively have the power to show us trends and truths we might not see otherwise. When building a collective of stories that we can learn from, the characters are important. Who is telling the stories (and to what audience)? Whose voices are amplified? Whose voices are silenced? How might the missing voices change or trouble our current understandings?

In Chapter 5, Mikkaka Overstreet shared stories from her efforts to forge relationships in a clinical partnership setting followed by a chapter by Tammi Davis featuring the stories of four PSTs that offer a vital perspective on the impact of school-university partnerships and the role narrative plays in their reflective practice as they develop a teaching repertoire.

CONCLUSION

2.4 Reflective Action

In 1983, Donald Schön wrote a seminal text titled, *The Reflective Practitioner*, where he descripted the act of reflection-in-action and how an individual continues to refine their practice through an act of "improvisation" or in other words, a metacognitive approach to our practice. Teaching is an art form that a practitioner refines throughout their career. To do so, that teacher must reflect on their instruction, their students' progress, and the needs and strengths of their contexts. Reflection alone, however, is not enough. Reflection without action is much like wishing without effort. Growth and change cannot come about without action. In the rationale for CAEP Standard 2, educator preparation programs are exhorted to develop field experiences that "offer multiple opportunities for candidates to develop, practice, demonstrate, and *reflect* upon clinical and academic components of preparation, *as well as* opportunities to *develop, practice, and demonstrate* evidence-based, pedagogical practices" (CAEP, 2019, emphasis added). In Chapter 7, Bianca Nightengale-Lee guided us through her efforts to push her PSTs to be more reflective about their own intersectional identities and those of K-12 students. This inquiry is followed by the case story of Emily Zuccaro in Chapter 8 where she considers how this reflection becomes active: how does the reflective work impact PSTs thoughts, beliefs, and values and how, in turn, does that affect how they talk about children? On the journey to ideological becoming, our PSTs use active, reflective practice to then become researchers in their own classrooms. That is taking up inquiry as a stance to understand the complexities of teaching and learning in urban settings.

2.5 Inquiry as Stance

Up to this point, our model (Figure 10.1) situates the need of students to explore their multiple identities, the relationships that they build with children, families, and teachers, how those relationships create narratives and stories that support the ongoing ideological becoming of PSTs as they engage in reflective action. Now, our PSTs engage in the act of inquiry. CAEP Standard 2 calls for PSTs to, through field experiences, conduct research and become innovators and problem solvers (CAEP, 2019). Building on the work of Marilyn Cochran-Smith and Susan Lytle (2009), we situate the work, assignments, projects, readings, and engagements as an act of inquiry. In other words, we engage our PSTs in the act of questioning that is fueled by the act of inquiry—collecting data, analyzing the data, and writing as well as presenting their findings situating that thinking in theoretical underpinning about the act of teaching and learning. Emily Zuccaro in Chapter 8 explores the discourse practices of her PSTs and creates a space for them to engage in a deep analysis of literacy practices and dialogic pedagogy. Also, Anetria Swanson details a documentary account of a first-year teacher and along with his ongoing inquiry about the act of teaching and learning. The teacher and Swanson dig deeply and theoretically about inquiry as stance helping both to understand the messy reality of urban partnerships. Finally, in our model, the act of inquiry as stance leads to the act of negotiation and argument that is critical to the path of ideological becoming.

2.6 Argument

What is the importance of argument in the preparation of teachers in urban clinical partnerships? Argument at its very core is the act of negotiation. Questioning known knowledge. Challenging historical thinking. Presenting a rebuttal of widely held beliefs including deficit orientations to children who present difference—difference in learning abilities, poverty, beliefs, race, language, and culture. As our PSTs grow in their multiple identities, perspectives, stories, relationships, reflective practice, and engaging in the act of inquiry as stance, now our PSTs begin to negotiate new understandings and engage in argument to challenge new thinking about the act of teaching and learning.

An example of the role of negotiation or argument in the act of teaching is illuminated in Chapter 9 where Anetria Swanson challenges us to think about how partnerships matter when teachers move from a preservice program into the field by building a relationship with Swanson as he challenges widely held practices that he sees as inhibiting his students' growth. She asked tough questions about the effectiveness of teacher education programs and about how districts and schools support first-year teachers. Taking up a different perspective on argument, Lori Norton Meier in Chapter 3 situates the work of college professors who create a "third space" where they can exist in a place where challenging the status quo and traditional forms of teacher education using argument in these third spaces to ask PSTs to think deeply noting that there are no easy answers—only safe environments to debate and challenge the messy reality of teaching and learning.

3 Putting the Model into Action

Throughout the chapters of this text, each chapter author shared another story of the messy reality of this work of preparing teachers in urban partnership settings. However, with all the stories of what didn't work we also heard important threads throughout that create a firm foundation to live the model and put it into action in our future endeavors. We describe four critical threads in the following paragraphs.

3.1 *Emotions and Relationships Set Any Standard*

It may seem strange to begin by asking the reader to recognize that learning is emotional. Although emotion may not appear in any standard, goal, objective, or sequencing guide, emotion is central to learning. Throughout the chapters, the authors described professional narratives of children and preservice teachers who described joy, frustration, sorrow, worry, intrigue, shock, delight, just to name a few. This emotion emerged from the situated context of relationships. Without a recognition of emotion and relationships in teaching and learning, urban clinical partnerships will struggle to reach the impact and potential to transform our spaces for all involved.

3.2 *Mediating Artifacts*

The use of the term "mediating" comes from the thinking of Lev Vygotsky (1978). We use the term mediating artifacts to consider what assignments, readings, and learning opportunities do we make available that act as a "mediator" for our student's learning? Mediating artifacts exist as a space for moving between the known and new, the university and the school, from being a student to becoming a teacher.

3.3 *Teaching as an Act of Inquiry*

Throughout each professional narrative written by a chapter author in this text, not only does the university instructor see teaching as an act of inquiry but she or he also sets up the classroom not as a didactic lecture course but where teaching becomes an act of inquiry. It is in this act of inquiry that we move beyond the classroom dedicated to our students and out into the elementary school where we ask questions about problems related to practice. We demonstrate for the PSTs that no act of teaching is perfect but if we engage in an act of inquiry driven by theory, research, and practice, then we engage a way of being in the world that we are always learning to better understand the teaching and learning dynamic.

3.4 *Not Fearing the Argument*

Finally, each chapter author makes an argument, engages an argument, and asks the reader to consider the argument. We also make the act of argument open, available, and encouraged for our students. To question the status quo. To challenge a research article. To engage a conversation with a peer about if a shared elementary student is actually learning. To debate what theory really looks like in the very schools where we situate this work. The messy reality about the spaces where we do this work is that there is no easy answer to some of the most complex problems children, families, teachers, and university partners face, however we cannot be complacent or be afraid to engage in the negotiation of argument that will push us to seek out complex solutions to these perplexing, persisting issues.

4   Final Words of a "Preservice Teacher"

> Hi, my name is Amyara. Let's be mermaids! (Amyara, Age 7 to her university writing buddy)

> My time with Amyara is coming to an end. From the first day she asked me to be a mermaid with her until today, I think how much we both have changed. I started this project asking the question, "How will I help her to become a better writer?" Then, I asked questions about her spelling and her inventions. Now, my questions are about how the time that we spent together helped her creativity flow and is there a way to measure how her confidence has grown in who she is as a writer. I feel more and more like a teacher sitting beside Amyara but it isn't because I have the perfect formula for writing instruction but that I know that I have to continually sit beside each child and ask the question, "what can I do to help you grow as a writer today?" (Written reflection by Ellyn, a junior in early childhood education)

We end this story where it began ... with the words of a child and her university preservice teacher. In their words and reflections, we hear identity, a relationship, their unique story, reflective action to inform writing instruction and learning, questions that push Ellyn to take an inquiry stance, and a new emerging argument from her challenging her earlier thinking with a new revelation about what is truly at the heart of her writing teaching and the growth she sees in Amyara as a writer.

We reiterate that this work is messy and we invite the reader to join is in the investigations of not only what works in urban clinical partnerships but also the layers of the messy reality that make this work worthwhile. This is not "THE END" but always this: To be continued ...

References

American Association of Colleges for Teacher Education (AACTE) Clinical Practice Commission. (2018). *A pivot toward clinical practice, its Lexicon, and the renewal of educator preparation.*

Bakhtin, M. (1981). *The dialogic imagination* (M. Holquist, Ed.). Austin, TX: University of Texas Press.

Bakhtin, M. M., & Medvedev, P. N. (1978). *The formal method in literary scholarship: A critical introduction to sociological poetics* (A. J. Wehrle, Trans.). Baltimore, MD: John Hopkins University Press. (Original work published 1928)

Cochran-Smith, M., & Lytle, S. (2009). *Inquiry as stance: Practitioner research for the next generation.* New York, NY: Teachers College Press.

Council for the Accreditation of Educator Preparation. (2019, September 30). Standard 2: Clinical partnerships and practice. Retrieved from http://caepnet.org/standards/standard-2

Love, B. L. (2015). What is Hip-Hop-based education doing in nice fields such as early childhood and elementary education? *Urban Education, 50*(1), 106–131. doi:10.1177/0042085914563182

Moje, E. B., & Luke, A. (2009). Literacy and identity: Examining the metaphors in history and contemporary research. *Reading Research Quarterly, 44*(4), 415–437.

Schön, D. (1983). *The reflective practitioner: How professionals think in action.* New York, NY: Basic Books.

Smagorinsky, P. (2018). Literacy in teacher education: "It's the context, stupid." *Journal of Literacy Research, 50*(3), 281–303. doi:10.1177/1086296X18784692

Tschida, C. M., Ryan, C. L., & Ticknor, A. S. (2014). Building on windows and mirrors: Encouraging the disruption of "single stories" through children's literature. *Journal of Children's Literature, 40*(1), 28–39.

Vygotsky, L. V. (1978). *The mind in society.* Cambridge, MA: Harvard University Press.

Printed in the United States
By Bookmasters